COOKIES FOR CHRISTMAS

By Jennifer Dorland Darling

Meredith® Press
An imprint of Meredith® Books

All of us at Meredith® Books are dedicated to providing you with the information and ideas you need to create delicious foods. We welcome your comments and suggestions. Write to us at: Meredith® Books, Cookbook Editorial Department, 1716 Locust St., Des Moines, IA 50309-3023.

If you would like to purchase any of our books, check wherever quality books are sold.

Our seal assures you that every recipe in *Cookies for Christmas* has been tested in the Better Homes and Gardens® Test Kitchen. This means that each recipe is practical and reliable, and meets our high standards of taste appeal. We guarantee your satisfaction with this book for as long as you own it.

Pictured on front cover:
Top left: Snickerdoodle Pinwheels (page 98)
Top right: Sugar Cookie Ornaments (page 196)
Bottom: Lemon-Almond Tea Cookies (page 167), Chocolate-Mint Thumbprints (page 166), Santa's Whiskers (page 164)

Meredith® Press
An imprint of Meredith® Books

COOKIES FOR CHRISTMAS

Editor: Jennifer Dorland Darling
Writers: Lisa Kingsley, Mary Major Williams, Winifred Moranville
Recipe Developers: Abby Dodge, Connie Hay, Shelli McConnell, Janet Pittman, Sarah Reynolds
Recipe Editor: Joyce Trollope
Graphic Designer: Craig Hanken
Copy Chief: Catherine Hamrick
Copy and Production Editor: Terri Fredrickson
Contributing Copy Editor: Jennifer Speer Ramundt
Contributing Proofreaders: Susan J. Kling, Sheila Mauck, Gretchen Kauffman
Electronic Production Coordinator: Paula Forest
Editorial and Design Assistants: Judy Bailey, Mary Lee Gavin, Karen Schirm
Test Kitchen Director: Sharon Stilwell
Test Kitchen Product Supervisor: Jill Hoefler
Food Stylists: Lynn Blanchard, Dianna Nolin, Jennifer Peterson
Photographers: Peter Krumhardt, Andy Lyons
Prop Stylist: Karen Johnson
Production Director: Douglas M. Johnston
Production Manager: Pam Kvitne
Assistant Prepress Manager: Marjorie J. Schenkelberg

Meredith® Books
Editor in Chief: James D. Blume
Design Director: Matt Strelecki
Managing Editor: Gregory H. Kayko

Director, Sales & Marketing, Retail: Michael A. Peterson
Director, Sales & Marketing, Special Markets: Rita McMullen
Director, Sales & Marketing, Home & Garden Center Channel: Ray Wolf
Director, Operations: George A. Susral

Vice President, General Manager: Jamie L. Martin

Meredith Publishing Group
President, Publishing Group: Christopher M. Little
Vice President, Consumer Marketing & Development: Hal Oringer

Meredith Corporation
Chairman and Chief Executive Officer: William T. Kerr

Chairman of the Executive Committee: E. T. Meredith III

DEAR CHRISTMAS COOKIE LOVER:

Anyone who loves to bake knows that baking Christmas cookies is about much more than the resulting goodies. For many, it's a chance to unwind while working with one's hands to transform a few simple ingredients into something magical in their beauty, warmth, and ability to capture the joys of the season. For others, it's a chance to prepare gifts that come straight from the heart—a symbol of the sweetness of friendship and family.

For me, baking is about all these things—but it's about family tradition, too. I trace my family's love of baking to my great-grandmother, who brought many of our family's favorite cookie recipes with her when she emigrated from Denmark to America.

Each Christmas season, no matter how busy my schedule as a food editor becomes, I take time out for a weekend of baking cookies with my mom. Together, we turn my kitchen into a cookie factory, baking batch after batch of our favorites, including decorated cutout cookies, sliced icebox cookies, and thumbprint cookies but always trying out a few new recipes, too. I cherish this weekend, for not only does it bring us a glorious stock of cookies to send to family near and far, but it also gives the two of us a chance to share good times while we remember the great cooks in our family who baked these same recipes for family and friends.

Carrying on the tradition of holiday baking is important to me. With a view toward passing this tradition to the next generation of cookie chefs, I've designated which recipes will be especially fun to bake with children. These are selected either because they offer kid-friendly steps in their preparation, or because they have fanciful shapes and designs children will love.

Though *Cookies for Christmas* possesses the homespun goodness of heirloom recipes, you don't have to be a veteran baker to prepare them yourself. I take great pride in having worked with the Better Homes and Gardens® Test Kitchen to ensure that each recipe meets their high standards of reliability and taste appeal. I'm confident that each will give you the expertise and information you need to make your own holiday baking successful and enjoyable.

With my best wishes for a season of home-baked goodness—and the bounty of family and friends to enjoy the sweet results,

Jennifer Dorland Darling

TABLE OF CONTENTS

CUTOUTS FOR CHRISTMAS

shimmering citrus snowflakes

ingredients

½ cup butter, softened

⅓ cup shortening

1 cup granulated sugar

⅓ cup dairy sour cream

1 egg

1 teaspoon vanilla

2 teaspoons finely shredded lemon peel (optional)

½ teaspoon finely shredded lime peel (optional)

¾ teaspoon baking powder

¼ teaspoon baking soda

Dash salt

2½ cups all-purpose flour

Assorted colors of edible glitter or colored sugar

Sifted powdered sugar

No two snowflakes are alike, and the same goes for these citrus-infused sweets. A simple drinking straw is as fancy a tool as you'll need to give each cookie its one-of-a-kind pattern, making it easy for kids to help.

Prep: 40 minutes   Chill: 2 hours   Bake: 7 to 8 minutes

1. In a large mixing bowl beat butter and shortening with an electric mixer on medium to high speed for 30 seconds. Add granulated sugar, sour cream, egg, vanilla, lemon and lime peels (if using), baking powder, baking soda, and salt. Beat until combined, scraping sides of bowl occasionally. Beat in as much of the flour as you can. Stir in remaining flour. Divide dough in half. Cover and chill about 2 hours or until easy to handle.

2. On a lightly floured surface, roll half of the dough at a time to ⅛- to ¼-inch thickness. Using cookie cutters or a sharp knife dipped in flour, cut dough into circles, triangles, squares, and/or diamonds. Using straws or aspic or hors d'oeuvre cutters, cut random holes in the cutout shapes so they resemble snowflakes. Use a straw to cut half circles from the edges to flute them. Using a wide spatula, place cookies about 1 inch apart on an ungreased cookie sheet. Sprinkle with edible cake glitter or colored sugar.

3. Bake in a 375° oven for 7 to 8 minutes or until edges are firm and bottoms are very lightly browned. Transfer cookies to a wire rack; cool. When cookies are cool, sprinkle with powdered sugar. Makes about 40 (2½-inch) cookies.

Nutrition facts per cookie: 87 cal., 5 g total fat (2 g sat. fat), 12 mg chol., 44 mg sodium, 11 g carbo., 0 g fiber, 1 g pro.

cookies with sparkle

Transform plain cookies into sparkling jewels with colored sugar and edible glitter.

• Decorate cookies with sugar immediately after rolling and cutting.

• Don't waste sugar by piling it on too thickly; only the sugar that touches the cookie dough will bake in place.

• To add texture, score the cookies lightly with a table knife.

Tie a bow atop a handled serving tray to share Shimmering Citrus Snowflakes with a friend. A snowflake doily handmade of parchment looks great as a tray liner. To make a parchment snowflake, fold a 13-inch square piece of parchment in half. Fold it in half again, bringing the folds together. Fold it one more time, bringing the folds together to form a triangle. Cut two even scallops along the unfolded edges; then use a small paper punch to create a design in the layered parchment.

spicy ginger houses

ingredients

¾ cup butter, softened

¾ cup packed brown sugar

2 tablespoons grated fresh ginger or 2 teaspoons ground ginger

1½ teaspoons finely ground black pepper

½ teaspoon baking soda

¼ teaspoon salt

¼ teaspoon ground cinnamon

¼ teaspoon ground nutmeg

1 egg

⅓ cup molasses

2¾ cups all-purpose flour

Red cinnamon candies or other small candies (optional)

1 recipe Royal Icing (see page 16) or purchased decorator icing (optional)

Black pepper is the secret ingredient in these sugar-and-spice cookies that make beautiful decorations. Serve them with milk to cool the tongue-tingling sensation they produce.

Prep: 50 minutes   Chill: 4 to 24 hours   Bake: 8 to 10 minutes

1. In a large mixing bowl beat butter with an electric mixer on medium to high speed for 30 seconds. Add brown sugar, ginger, pepper, baking soda, salt, cinnamon, and nutmeg; beat until combined, scraping sides of bowl occasionally. Beat in egg and molasses until combined. Beat in as much of the flour as you can with the mixer. Using a wooden spoon, stir in any remaining flour.

2. Divide dough in half. Cover and chill for 4 to 24 hours or until easy to handle.

3. Lightly grease a cookie sheet or line with parchment paper; set aside.

4. On a lightly floured surface, roll half of the dough at a time to ¼-inch thickness. Using a 6×4-inch house-shaped cookie cutter, cut out dough. Cut out small heart-shaped windows from houses, if desired. Cut additional hearts from scraps for decorations. Place house shapes on the prepared cookie sheet about 1 inch apart; place heart cutouts on a separate prepared cookie sheet because they may bake at a rate different from the house shapes.

5. Bake house shapes in a 350° oven about 10 minutes or until tops of cookies appear dry (bake heart shapes about 8 minutes). Cool on cookie sheet for 1 minute. Transfer cookies to a wire rack; cool.

6. When cookies are cool, decorate if desired with heart cutouts, candies, and icing, attaching candies and cutouts with the icing. Makes about 8 (6-inch) cookies.

Nutrition facts per 6-inch cookie without icing: 404 cal., 18 g total fat (11 g sat. fat), 73 mg chol., 204 mg sodium, 56 g carbo., 2 g fiber, 5 g pro.

10

black walnut thins

Piping the white icing in snowflake shapes atop these rich, nut-studded butter cookies puts on a holiday air.

Prep: 25 minutes   **Chill:** 2 hours   **Bake:** 8 to 10 minutes

1. In a large mixing bowl beat the butter with an electric mixer on medium to high speed for 30 seconds. Add the powdered sugar, vanilla, and salt. Beat until combined, scraping sides of bowl occasionally. Beat in the egg until combined. Beat in as much of the flour as you can with the mixer. Using a wooden spoon, stir in any remaining flour and the 1½ cups chopped nuts.

2. Divide dough in half. Cover and chill about 2 hours or until dough is easy to handle.

3. In a small bowl combine granulated sugar and the ½ cup chopped nuts; set aside.

4. On a lightly floured surface, roll half of the dough at a time to about ⅛-inch thickness. Using a 2½-inch round or fluted cookie cutter, cut into desired shapes.

Place cookies on an ungreased cookie sheet; sprinkle with the granulated sugar-nut mixture.

5. Bake in a 350° oven for 8 to 10 minutes or until bottoms are just golden brown. Cool on cookie sheet for 1 minute. Transfer cookies to a wire rack; cool. When cookies are cool, pipe on Powdered Sugar Icing in a snowflake pattern. Makes about 36 (2½-inch) cookies.

Powdered Sugar Icing: In a small mixing bowl stir together 1 cup sifted powdered sugar, ¼ teaspoon vanilla, and enough milk (2 to 4 teaspoons) to make of piping consistency.

Nutrition facts per cookie: 164 cal., 9 g total fat (3 g sat. fat), 20 mg chol., 33 mg sodium, 19 g carbo., 1 g fiber, 3 g pro.

ingredients

1 cup butter, softened

2¾ cups sifted powdered sugar

¾ teaspoon vanilla

¼ teaspoon salt

1 egg

2 cups all-purpose flour

1½ cups black walnuts or hazelnuts (filberts), toasted and chopped

½ cup granulated sugar

½ cup black walnuts or hazelnuts (filberts), toasted and finely chopped

1 recipe Powdered Sugar Icing

Give away a forest of these tiny Green Cherry Trees or pass them out individually. Wrap each tree in a cellophane bag along with a little shredded mylar for added sparkle. Tie the top closed and add a gift tag or slip a tiny cookie cutter over the top.

green cherry trees

Get the big kids in your house rolling and cutting, and let the littler ones decorate these three-dimensional sweet trees. (If they're not gobbled up right away, add them to a gingerbread house display.)

Prep: 45 minutes   Chill: 30 minutes to 1 hour   Bake: 12 to 14 minutes

ingredients

1 8-ounce jar green maraschino cherries (about 1 cup), well drained and finely chopped

2½ cups all-purpose flour

½ cup sugar

1 cup butter

Green paste food coloring

1 cup white baking pieces

2 teaspoons butter-flavor or regular shortening

Small multicolored decorative candies

1. Place chopped cherries in a fine sieve and squeeze out excess liquid; set aside.

2. In a large mixing bowl stir together flour and sugar. Using a pastry blender, cut in butter until mixture resembles coarse crumbs and starts to cling. Stir in cherries and a small amount of green paste food coloring. Form mixture into a ball and knead until well combined and nearly smooth.

3. Divide dough in half. If necessary, cover and chill dough for 30 minutes to 1 hour or until easy to handle.

4. On a lightly floured surface, roll half of the dough at a time to ¼- to ⅜-inch thickness. For each tree, cut dough using a 1-inch star cookie cutter (for the treetop) and 4 star cookie cutters that gradually increase in size from 2½ to 4 inches. Place cookies 1 inch apart on an ungreased cookie sheet.

5. Bake in a 325° oven 12 minutes for smaller stars and 14 minutes for larger stars or until bottoms are lightly browned. Transfer cookies to a wire rack; cool.

6. In a heavy small saucepan heat white baking pieces and shortening over low heat, stirring frequently, just until melted.

7. To assemble each tree, stack 5 stars, one of each size, with the largest on the bottom and the smallest standing on edge on the top. Spread a little of the melted white baking pieces mixture between cookies as you stack them. Drizzle or pipe melted white baking pieces mixture over each tree. Sprinkle with decorative candies. Makes about 6 cookie trees (depending on cutter sizes).

Nutrition facts per half tree: 363 cal., 21 g total fat (13 g sat. fat), 46 mg chol., 171 mg sodium, 41 g carbo., 1 g fiber, 4 g pro.

cactus cookies

ingredients

½ cup shortening

¼ cup butter, softened

½ cup granulated sugar

¼ cup packed brown sugar

1½ to 2 teaspoons anise seed, crushed

1 teaspoon baking powder

¼ teaspoon salt

1 egg yolk

2 tablespoons milk

1 teaspoon vanilla

2 cups all-purpose flour

1 recipe Powdered Sugar Icing

Food coloring

Purchased decorator icing

In some parts of the country, a Christmas tree may be a cactus strung with lights. To show off the anise seed cactus needles in these cookies, simply decorate with lights and flowers of frosting.

Prep: 35 minutes   Chill: 1 to 2 hours   Bake: 6 to 8 minutes

1. In a large mixing bowl beat shortening and butter with an electric mixer on medium to high speed for 30 seconds. Add granulated sugar, brown sugar, anise seed, baking powder, and salt. Beat until combined, scraping sides of bowl occasionally. Beat in egg yolk, milk, and vanilla until combined. Beat in as much of the flour as you can with the mixer. Using a wooden spoon, stir in any remaining flour.

2. Divide dough in half. Cover and chill for 1 to 2 hours or until dough is easy to handle.

3. On a lightly floured surface, roll half of the dough at a time to ¼-inch thickness. Using a 2½- to 3-inch cactus-shaped cookie cutter, cut out dough. Or, trace a cactus shape on paper and cut out; place the paper pattern on dough and cut around it with a sharp knife. Place cutouts on an ungreased cookie sheet.

4. Bake in a 375° oven for 6 to 8 minutes or until edges are lightly browned. Transfer cookies to a wire rack; cool.

5. When cookies are cool, divide Powdered Sugar Icing and tint a generous portion with green food coloring. Spread green icing on top of baked cookies. Tint remaining icing with red, purple, and yellow food coloring and use to pipe on a string of lights. Using red and green tinted decorator icing and a star tip, pipe a few flowers and leaves on each cactus; add a dot of frosting in the opposite color to the center of each flower, if desired. Makes about 30 (2½- to 3-inch) cookies.

Powdered Sugar Icing: In a medium mixing bowl stir together 2 cups sifted powdered sugar, ½ teaspoon orange extract, and 2 tablespoons milk. Stir in additional milk, 1 teaspoon at a time, to make icing of piping consistency.

Nutrition facts per cookie: 120 cal., 5 g total fat (2 g sat. fat), 11 mg chol., 47 mg sodium, 18 g carbo., 0 g fiber, 1 g pro.

mocha stars

What's the secret to these coffee-and-chocolate-flavored cookies? Would you believe a touch of cocoa powder and flecks of ground espresso beans! Enjoy them with—what else?—a great cup of coffee.

Prep: 35 minutes   Chill: 4 hours   Bake: 8 minutes

1. In a medium mixing bowl beat butter with an electric mixer on medium to high speed for 30 seconds. Add the brown sugar, ground espresso beans, cocoa powder, and salt. Beat until combined, scraping sides of bowl occasionally. Beat in egg yolk and coffee liqueur until combined. Beat in as much flour as you can with the mixer. Using a wooden spoon, stir in any remaining flour.

2. Divide dough in half. Cover and chill about 4 hours or until dough is easy to handle.

3. On a lightly floured surface, roll half of the dough at a time to ⅛- to ¼-inch thickness. Using various sizes of star-shaped cookie cutters, cut out dough. Place 1 inch apart on an ungreased cookie sheet.

4. Bake in a 350° oven about 8 minutes or until tops look dry. Cool on cookie sheet for 1 minute. Transfer cookies to a wire rack; cool.

5. If desired, in a heavy small saucepan combine chocolate pieces and shortening; stir over medium-low heat until melted. Dip some of the star points into melted chocolate. Makes about 36 (2-inch) cookies.

Nutrition facts per undipped cookie: 53 cal., 3 g total fat (2 g sat. fat), 13 mg chol., 5 mg sodium, 6 g carbo., 0 g fiber, 1 g pro.

ingredients

½ cup butter, softened

½ cup packed light brown sugar

2 teaspoons finely ground espresso beans, sifted

2 teaspoons unsweetened cocoa powder

   Dash salt

1 egg yolk

1 tablespoon coffee liqueur

1½ cups all-purpose flour

¾ cup semisweet chocolate pieces (optional)

1 tablespoon shortening (optional)

gingerbread cutouts

ingredients

2½ cups all-purpose flour

1 cup whole wheat flour

1 teaspoon ground
cinnamon

1 teaspoon ground ginger

¾ teaspoon baking soda

½ teaspoon ground nutmeg

¼ teaspoon salt

¼ teaspoon ground cloves

1 cup butter, softened

1 cup granulated sugar

1 egg

½ cup molasses

2 tablespoons lemon juice

1 recipe Royal Icing

Food coloring

Small candies for
decorating

Santa and his helpers, stars, reindeer, or scampering gingerbread kids—there's no limit to the Christmas images you can make with this timeless cutout cookie recipe.

Prep: 40 minutes   Chill: 3 hours   Bake: 8 to 10 minutes

1. In a medium bowl stir together all-purpose and whole wheat flours, cinnamon, ginger, baking soda, nutmeg, salt, and cloves; set aside.

2. In a large mixing bowl beat butter with an electric mixer on medium to high speed for 30 seconds. Add sugar; beat until fluffy. Beat in egg until mixture is light. Beat in molasses and lemon juice on low speed until combined. Beat in as much of flour mixture as you can with the mixer. Stir in any remaining flour mixture.

3. Divide dough in half. Cover and chill at least 3 hours or until dough is easy to handle.

4. On a lightly floured surface, roll half of the dough at a time to ⅛-inch thickness. Using cookie cutters, cut out dough. (For Santas, use tear-drop-shaped cookie cutters of various sizes.) Place 1 inch apart on an ungreased cookie sheet.

5. Bake in a 350° oven for 8 to 10 minutes or until edges are lightly browned. Cool

on cookie sheet for 1 minute. Transfer cookies to a wire rack; cool. When cookies are cool, decorate with white or tinted Royal Icing and candies. Makes about 90 (2½-inch) cookies.

Royal Icing: In a medium mixing bowl combine 2 cups sifted powdered sugar and 4 teaspoons meringue powder.* Add 3 tablespoons cold water. Beat with an electric mixer on low speed until mixture is combined; then beat on medium to high speed for 5 to 8 minutes or until mixture forms stiff peaks. (If mixture seems stiff while beating, add water, ½ teaspoon at a time. Icing should be fairly thick for piping. For a thinner glazing consistency, stir in a little more water after beating.) When not using, keep tightly covered to prevent it from drying out; keep refrigerated. Makes 2 cups.

Note: Look for meringue powder at kitchen, cake-decorating, and crafts shops.

Nutrition facts per cookie: 57 cal., 2 g total fat (1 g sat. fat), 8 mg chol., 38 mg sodium, 9 g carbo., 0 g fiber, 1 g pro.

These jolly elves are right at home snuggled in a box with snowlike crinkled white paper and a few candy canes. Tie up this box of cheer using pieces of red and green cording with jingle bells dangling from the ends. Gingerbread Cutouts—in any shape—make whimsical gift tags when the recipient's name is piped in icing on the cookie. To turn cookies into gift tags, before baking just use a drinking straw to poke a hole in the top big enough for threading a ribbon through later.

pastry pillows

ingredients

- 2 cups all-purpose flour
- ¼ teaspoon salt
- 1 cup butter, cut up
- 1 8-ounce package cream cheese, cut up

  Apricot, peach, raspberry, strawberry, or cherry preserves

  Almond paste
- 1 beaten egg
- 1 tablespoon water

  Coarse or pearl sugar

*A **cream cheese dough** is the key to these soft, flaky, filled cookies. Choose your favorite preserves for the filling.*

Prep: 40 minutes **Chill:** 1 hour **Bake:** 10 to 12 minutes

1. In a food processor bowl* combine flour and salt. Cover and process until mixed. Add the butter and cream cheese. Cover and process until well combined. (Or, in a medium mixing bowl beat softened butter and cream cheese with an electric mixer until combined. Add flour and salt; beat on low speed of mixer just until combined.)

2. Divide dough in half. Cover and chill at least 1 hour or until dough is easy to handle.

3. On lightly floured surface, roll half of the dough at a time to ⅛-inch thickness. Cut dough into 2-inch squares. Place half of the dough squares on an ungreased cookie sheet. Place a scant ¼ teaspoon each of preserves and almond paste in the center of each square.

4. Combine beaten egg and water. Brush edges of layered squares with egg mixture. Top each layered square with a plain dough square. Lightly press edges together, then seal all edges with tines of a fork.

Brush filled and sealed dough squares with egg mixture. Sprinkle lightly with coarse or pearl sugar.

5. Bake in a 375° oven for 10 to 12 minutes or until golden. Transfer cookies to a wire rack; cool. Makes about 52 (2-inch) cookies.

Note: If using a small-capacity food processor, mix half of the ingredients at a time.

Nutrition facts per cookie: 74 cal., 5 g total fat (3 g sat. fat), 18 mg chol., 61 mg sodium, 5 g carbo., 0 g fiber, 1 g pro.

18

eggnog angels

Kids will adore making their own decorations of nutmeg-spiced heavenly hosts whose "stained glass" windows are simply crushed hard candies that melt during baking and reharden when cool.

Prep: 40 minutes   **Chill:** 2 hours   **Bake:** 7 to 9 minutes

1. In a bowl stir together flour, sugar, baking powder, and nutmeg. Using a pastry blender, cut in butter until pieces are size of small peas. Make a well in center. Mix together egg and milk; add all at once to flour mixture. Using a wooden spoon, stir until dough is moistened. Gently knead in bowl until combined.* Divide dough in half. Cover and chill about 2 hours.

2. Line a cookie sheet with foil; set aside. On a lightly floured surface, roll half of the dough at a time to ⅛-inch thickness (keep remaining dough refrigerated). Using a 3- or 5½-inch angel-shaped cookie cutter, cut out dough. Place angels 1 inch apart on prepared cookie sheet.

3. If making 3-inch angels, cut a bell from center of angel using a 1½-inch bell-shaped cookie cutter. If making 5½-inch angels, cut 2 bells from bottom of angel using a 1½-inch bell-shaped cookie cutter. Fill bell cutouts with crushed candies, using about ¼ to ½ teaspoon candy per bell. If desired, sprinkle with edible glitter.

4. Bake in a 375° oven for 7 to 9 minutes or until edges are firm and lightly browned. Cool on cookie sheet for 1 minute. Transfer cookies to a wire rack; cool. If desired, decorate angels by piping on Powdered Sugar Icing. Makes about 48 (3-inch) or 16 (5-inch) angel cookies.

Powdered Sugar Icing: In a small bowl stir together 1 cup sifted powdered sugar and enough milk (about 2 to 3 teaspoons) to make icing of piping consistency.

Note: To prepare dough using a large food processor, place flour, sugar, baking powder, and nutmeg in the food processor bowl. Cover and process until mixed. Add pieces of butter. Cover and process with several on/off turns until the mixture forms fine crumbs. Mix egg and milk; add to flour mixture. Cover and process until mixture is just moistened. Continue as above, beginning at step 2.

Nutrition facts per 3-inch cookie: 63 cal., 3 g total fat (2 g sat. fat), 11 mg chol., 34 mg sodium, 9 g carbo., 0 g fiber, 1 g pro.

ingredients

- 2 cups all-purpose flour
- ¾ cup granulated sugar
- ¾ teaspoon baking powder
- ½ teaspoon ground nutmeg
- ⅔ cup butter, cut up
- 1 beaten egg
- 2 tablespoons milk
- ⅔ to 1 cup crushed hard candies
- Edible glitter (optional)
- 1 recipe Powdered Sugar Icing (optional)

Nestle Browned Butter Animals in a snowfall of sugar inside a wide-mouth, clear glass jar for a charming gift. If you'd like, add polka-dot snowflakes to the outside of the jar using a round-tip pencil eraser or the end of an artist's paintbrush dipped in white glass paint. For a Christmas party take-home treat, stand a cookie in a sugar-filled margarita glass and wrap the glass stem in a candy cane stripe of red and white pipe cleaners. Place a filled and decorated glass by each guest's plate.

browned butter animals

Buerre noisette—*the French term for butter that has been cooked to a light hazelnut color—lends a rich, nutty flavor to these not-too-sweet pastrylike cookies.*

Prep: 40 minutes   Chill: 45 minutes   Bake: 6 to 8 minutes

1. In a heavy small saucepan melt butter over low heat. Continue heating until butter turns a rich golden brown, stirring occasionally. Remove from heat. Pour into a small bowl and chill about 45 minutes or until firm, stirring occasionally.

2. In a large mixing bowl combine flour, brown sugar, baking powder, and salt. Remove the browned butter from the small bowl discarding any watery liquid at the bottom of the bowl. Place the solid brown butter in the flour mixture. Cut the butter into the flour until pieces are the size of small peas.

3. Stir together the egg yolks and 2 tablespoons of the milk. Gradually stir into flour mixture. Add remaining milk, 1 tablespoon at a time, until all the dough is moistened. If necessary, gently knead dough just until a ball forms.

4. On a lightly floured surface, roll half of the dough at a time to ¼-inch thickness. Using 3-inch animal-shaped cookie cutters, cut out dough. Place on an ungreased cookie sheet.

5. Bake in a 425° oven for 6 to 8 minutes or until golden brown. Cool on wire racks. Pipe Powdered Sugar Icing to outline and add detail to the animals. Makes 32 (3-inch) cookies.

Powdered Sugar Icing: In a medium mixing bowl stir together 2 cups sifted powdered sugar and 2 tablespoons milk. Stir in additional milk, 1 teaspoon at a time, to make icing of piping consistency. Tint icing with paste food coloring, if desired.

Nutrition facts per cookie: 117 cal., 6 g total fat (4 g sat. fat), 29 mg chol., 80 mg sodium, 15 g carbo., 0 g fiber, 1 g pro.

ingredients

- 1 cup butter
- 2½ cups all-purpose flour
- ¼ cup firmly packed brown sugar
- ¼ teaspoon baking powder
- ¼ teaspoon salt
- 2 beaten egg yolks
- 5 to 7 tablespoons milk
- 1 recipe Powdered Sugar Icing

vanilla snowflakes

The scent of vanilla evokes feelings of comfort and home. Starting with a whole vanilla bean gives these apple jelly-filled cookies incomparable flavor and a comfortable, homey aroma.

ingredients

1   vanilla bean

2   tablespoons milk

1   cup butter, softened

1¼   cups granulated sugar

1½   teaspoons baking powder

    Dash salt

4   egg yolks or 2 eggs

3   cups all-purpose flour

½   cup apple jelly

3   tablespoons coarse sugar

Prep: 40 minutes   Chill: 1 to 2 hours   Bake: 8 to 10 minutes

1. Split the vanilla bean lengthwise and scrape out and reserve the seeds; cut the pod into 1-inch lengths. In a microwave-safe small bowl combine the seeds, pod pieces, and milk. Microwave, uncovered, on 100% power (high) about 30 seconds or until milk just begins to boil. Cool to room temperature. Remove the vanilla pod pieces and discard. Reserve the milk and seed mixture.

2. In a large mixing bowl beat butter with an electric mixer on medium to high speed for 30 seconds. Add granulated sugar, baking powder, and salt. Beat until combined, scraping sides of bowl occasionally. Beat in the egg yolks or eggs and milk mixture until combined. Beat in as much of the flour as you can with the mixer. Using a wooden spoon, stir in remaining flour.

3. Divide dough in half. If necessary, cover and chill dough for 1 to 2 hours or until it is easy to handle.

4. On a lightly floured surface, roll half of the dough at a time to ¼-inch thickness. Using a 1½- or 2-inch snowflake-shaped cookie cutter, cut out dough. Place on an ungreased cookie sheet. Make a slight depression in the center of each snowflake. (Use the back of a ¼ teaspoon measure to make the depression, if desired.) Spoon about ⅛ teaspoon jelly into each center. Sprinkle cookies generously with coarse sugar.

5. Bake in a 375° oven for 8 to 10 minutes or until edges are firm and bottoms are very lightly browned. Transfer cookies to a wire rack; cool. Makes about 180 (1½-inch) or 144 (2-inch) cookies.

Nutrition facts per 1½-inch cookie: 26 cal., 1 g total fat (1 g sat. fat), 7 mg chol., 15 mg sodium, 4 g carbo., 0 g fiber, 0 g pro.

almond galettes

In the vernacular of French cooking and baking, a galette *is simply a kind of cake. These little almond-infused "cakes" are the essence of simple sophistication.*

Prep: 30 minutes   Bake: 7 to 9 minutes

1. Lightly grease a cookie sheet; set aside.

2. Crumble almond paste into a large mixing bowl. Beat with an electric mixer on medium to high speed for 30 seconds. Add the butter and beat for 30 seconds more. Add the sugar, lemon peel, and the ½ teaspoon almond extract. Beat about 2 minutes more or until combined, scraping sides of bowl occasionally. Beat in as much flour as you can with the mixer. Using a wooden spoon, stir in any remaining flour. Divide dough in half.

3. On a lightly floured surface, roll half of the dough at a time to ¼-inch thickness. Using a 2-inch square scalloped cookie cutter, cut out dough. Place on prepared cookie sheet.

4. In a small bowl beat the egg yolks, water, and the ¼ teaspoon almond extract until combined. Brush the egg mixture onto cookies. Place 2 almond slices on each cookie.

5. Bake in a 375° oven for 7 to 9 minutes or until edges are firm and bottoms are very lightly browned. Cool on cookie sheet for 1 minute. Transfer cookies to a wire rack; cool. Makes about 36 (2-inch) cookies.

Nutrition facts per cookie: 114 cal., 7 g total fat (3 g sat. fat), 25 mg chol., 53 mg sodium, 11 g carbo., 0 g fiber, 2 g pro.

ingredients

- 1 8-ounce can almond paste
- 1 cup butter, softened
- ½ cup sugar
- 2 teaspoons finely shredded lemon peel
- ½ teaspoon almond extract
- 2 cups all-purpose flour
- 2 egg yolks
- 4 teaspoons water
- ¼ teaspoon almond extract
  Sliced almonds

biscochitos

ingredients

- 3 cups all-purpose flour
- 1½ teaspoons anise seed, crushed
- 1 teaspoon baking powder
- ½ teaspoon salt
- 1¼ cups butter-flavor shortening
- 1 egg
- ½ cup granulated sugar
- 3 tablespoons frozen orange juice concentrate, thawed, or brandy
- 1 teaspoon vanilla
- Cinnamon-sugar (optional)
- Crushed anise seed (optional)

Made at Christmastime throughout Mexico and the American Southwest, these anise-flavored "biscuits" are traditionally cut into birds, flowers, and other fanciful shapes.

Prep: 30 minutes   Bake: 9 minutes

1. Lightly grease a cookie sheet; set aside.

2. In a medium bowl stir together flour, the 1½ teaspoons anise seed, the baking powder, and salt; set aside.

3. In a large mixing bowl beat shortening with an electric mixer on medium speed until fluffy. Add egg, granulated sugar, orange juice concentrate or brandy, and vanilla. Beat until mixture is light. Beat in as much of the flour mixture as you can with the mixer. Using a wooden spoon, stir in any remaining flour mixture (dough will be stiff). Divide dough in half.

4. On a lightly floured surface, use a floured rolling pin to roll half of the dough at a time to ¼-inch thickness. Using a 2½-inch cookie cutter, cut dough into desired shapes. If desired, sprinkle cutouts with cinnamon-sugar and additional crushed anise seed. Place on prepared cookie sheet.

5. Bake in a 350° oven about 9 minutes or until bottoms are golden. Transfer to a wire rack; cool. Makes about 36 (2½-inch) cookies.

Nutrition facts per cookie: 114 cal., 7 g total fat (2 g sat. fat), 6 mg chol., 42 mg sodium, 11 g carbo., 0 g fiber, 1 g pro.

perfect cutouts

Round up your cookie cutters and follow these tips for effortless cookie baking.

- When rolling and cutting, work with half of the cookie dough at a time. Keep the other dough half refrigerated until you're ready to roll it out.
- Keep the dough from sticking to the countertop or pastry cloth by lightly sprinkling the surface with all-purpose flour.
- Dip the cutter in flour between uses to keep dough from sticking to it.
- Combine any scraps of dough and reroll on a very lightly floured surface. Handle and roll the dough as little as possible to keep the cookies tender.

A bushel of fruit-shaped Biscochitos look as sweet as can be packed up in a small wooden crate lined with a fruit motif fabric napkin. Try embellishing the box with a bow of tiny artificial fruits (found at crafts and discount stores).

special sugar cookie cutouts

ingredients

- ⅓ cup butter, softened
- ⅓ cup shortening
- ¾ cup sugar
- 1 teaspoon baking powder
- Dash salt
- 1 egg
- 1 teaspoon vanilla
- 2 cups all-purpose flour
- Paste food coloring

Use as many colors of dough as you like—the decorating's done on these cookies before they even go in the oven! For a classic sugar cookie cutout, leave out the food coloring and special decorations.

Prep: 35 minutes   Chill: 1¼ hours   Bake: 7 to 10 minutes

1. In a medium mixing bowl beat butter and shortening with an electric mixer on medium to high speed for 30 seconds. Add sugar, baking powder, and salt. Beat until combined, scraping sides of bowl occasionally. Beat in egg and vanilla until combined. Beat in as much of the flour as you can with the mixer. Using a wooden spoon, stir in any remaining flour.

2. Divide dough into portions, tinting each portion of dough with a different color of food coloring. Knead coloring into dough until well mixed. Cover and chill about 1 hour or until dough is easy to handle.

3. On a lightly floured surface, roll a portion of the dough at a time to ⅛-inch thickness. Using a 2½-inch cookie cutter, cut dough into desired shapes. (For 5¼-inch cookies, roll dough to ¼-inch thickness.) Place cutouts on an ungreased cookie sheet. Refrigerate cutouts for 15 minutes. Using small cookie cutters, make smaller cutouts and fill each opening with another color of dough.

4. Bake in a 375° oven for 7 to 8 minutes for smaller cookies or about 10 minutes for larger cookies or until edges are firm and bottoms are very lightly browned. Cool on cookie sheet for 1 minute. Transfer cookies to a wire rack; cool. Makes about 48 (2½-inch) cookies or about 16 (5¼-inch) cookies.

Nutrition facts per 2½-inch cookie: 55 cal., 3 g total fat (1 g sat. fat), 8 mg chol., 25 mg sodium, 7 g carbo., 0 g fiber, 1 g pro.

peppermint cookie pops

Nostalgic for those "of a certain age" and pure delight to the younger set, these super-sized cookies on a stick are reminiscent of old-fashioned peppermint lollipops.

Prep: 2 hours   Chill: 3 hours   Bake: 8 to 10 minutes

1. In a large mixing bowl beat butter and shortening with an electric mixer on medium to high speed for 30 seconds. Add sugar, baking powder, and salt. Beat until combined, scraping sides of bowl occasionally. Add the eggs and peppermint extract; beat until well combined. Beat in as much of the flour as you can with the mixer. Using a wooden spoon, stir in any remaining flour and the peppermint candies.

2. Divide dough in half. Cover and chill about 3 hours or until dough is easy to handle.

3. On a lightly floured surface, roll half of the dough at a time to ¼-inch thickness. Using a 4-inch round scalloped cookie cutter, cut out dough. Place cookies about 1 inch apart on an ungreased cookie sheet. Tuck a lollipop stick under the center of each cookie. Press dough down slightly so that the cookie bakes around the stick.

4. Using a decorating bag fitted with a medium writing or star tip, pipe colored Decorating Dough onto cutouts, making borders, designs, or pictures and/or writing messages.

5. Bake in a 375° oven for 8 to 10 minutes or until edges are firm and bottoms are lightly browned. Cool on cookie sheet for 1 minute. Carefully transfer cookies to a wire rack; cool. Makes about 24 (4-inch) cookies.

Decorating Dough: In a medium mixing bowl beat ½ cup butter with an electric mixer on medium speed for 30 seconds. Add ½ cup sugar and beat until combined. With mixer on low speed, beat in ¾ cup half-and-half or light cream. Beat in 2 cups all-purpose flour until dough is smooth. Divide dough into portions. Tint dough with desired paste food coloring. Makes about 2⅓ cups dough.

Nutrition facts per cookie: 328 cal., 16 g total fat (8 g sat. fat), 44 mg chol., 153 mg sodium, 43 g carbo., 1 g fiber, 4 g pro.

ingredients

⅔ cup butter, softened
⅔ cup shortening
1½ cups sugar
2 teaspoons baking powder
¼ teaspoon salt
2 eggs
¼ teaspoon peppermint extract
4 cups all-purpose flour
½ cup finely crushed hard peppermint candies
24 lollipop sticks
1 recipe Decorating Dough

Tie up bundles of herbed Apricot-Sage Cookies with a bow and insert a sprig of fresh (for immediate giving) or dried (for later giving) sage or rosemary. To play up the fruit side of these treats, pack them in a small berry basket or wooden apple basket.

apricot-sage cookies

These jam-filled sandwich cookies—made crunchy with cornmeal—are an elegant holiday treat. For a different flavor, substitute rosemary or lemon thyme for the baked-in fresh sage.

Prep: 25 minutes   **Bake:** 7 minutes

1. In a medium mixing bowl stir together flour, sugar, and cornmeal. Using a pastry blender, cut in butter until mixture resembles fine crumbs and starts to cling. Stir in herb. Add milk and stir with a fork to combine. Form mixture into a ball and knead dough until smooth. Divide dough in half.

2. On a lightly floured surface, roll half of the dough at a time to ⅛-inch thickness. Using a 2½-inch round cookie cutter, cut out dough.

3. In a small bowl combine the egg white and water. Brush half of the cookies with the egg white mixture. Place a small sage leaf or two on each cookie, if desired.

Brush leaves with egg white mixture. Sprinkle with sugar. Place on an ungreased cookie sheet.

4. Bake in a 375° oven about 7 minutes or until edges are firm and bottoms are very lightly browned. Transfer cookies to a wire rack; cool.

5. Snip any large pieces of fruit in preserves. Spread apricot preserves on the bottom of each cookie without a sage leaf. Top preserves layer with a sage leaf-topped cookie, bottom side down. Makes 16 (2½-inch) sandwich cookies.

Nutrition facts per cookie: 130 cal., 6 g total fat (4 g sat. fat), 16 mg chol., 64 mg sodium, 18 g carbo., 0 g fiber, 2 g pro.

ingredients

- 1¾ cups all-purpose flour
- ⅓ cup sugar
- ¼ cup yellow cornmeal
- ½ cup butter
- 2 tablespoons snipped fresh sage, lemon thyme, or rosemary or 2 teaspoons dried sage or rosemary, crushed
- 3 tablespoons milk
- 1 egg white
- 1 tablespoon water
- Fresh sage leaves (optional)
- Sugar
- 2 tablespoons apricot preserves

macadamia nut cookies

ingredients

- 1 cup all-purpose flour
- 1 cup macadamia nuts, very finely chopped*
- ⅔ cup granulated sugar
- ½ cup butter
- 1 egg yolk
- 1 recipe Pineapple-Cream Cheese Frosting

Christmas in the tropics translates into terrific treats starring Hawaii's most celebrated nut. Top off the pineapple-cream cheese frosting with a pearllike strand of macadamias, if you like.

Prep: 40 minutes   Chill: 1 hour   Bake: 8 to 10 minutes

1. In a medium mixing bowl combine flour, nuts, and granulated sugar. Using a pastry blender, cut in butter until mixture resembles coarse crumbs. Stir in egg yolk. Knead dough until mixture forms a ball.

2. If necessary, cover and chill dough about 1 hour or until dough is easy to handle. Divide dough in half.

3. On a lightly floured surface, roll half of the dough at a time to ¼-inch thickness. Using a 2-inch cookie cutter, cut into desired shapes. Place on an ungreased cookie sheet.

4. Bake in a 350° oven for 8 to 10 minutes or until lightly browned on edges. Transfer cookies to a wire rack; cool. When cookies are cool, frost with Pineapple-Cream Cheese Frosting. Makes about 36 (2-inch) cookies.

Pineapple-Cream Cheese Frosting:
In a mixing bowl beat one 3-ounce package cream cheese and 3 tablespoons butter, softened, until combined. Beat in 1 cup sifted powdered sugar and 2 tablespoons pineapple preserves. Beat in 1 to 1¼ cups sifted powdered sugar to make frosting of spreading consistency.

*Note: If using a food processor to chop the nuts, be sure not to overprocess them to the point that they become nut butter. Use several on/off turns to process just until the nuts are very finely chopped.

Nutrition facts per cookie: 117 cal., 7 g total fat (3 g sat. fat), 18 mg chol., 43 mg sodium, 13 g carbo., 0 g fiber, 1 g pro.

mascarpone creams

The super-rich Italian cream cheese called mascarpone makes these delicate, chocolate-spread cookies elegant and festive. Sprinkle the cutout cookie tops with white nonpareils for extra flair.

Prep: 50 minutes   Chill: 1 to 2 hours   Bake: 5 to 7 minutes

1. Lightly grease 2 cookie sheets; set aside.

2. In a large mixing bowl beat butter with an electric mixer on medium to high speed for 30 seconds. Add granulated sugar, baking powder, nutmeg (if desired), baking soda, and salt. Beat until combined, scraping sides of bowl occasionally. Beat in the mascarpone cheese or sour cream and the egg. Beat in as much of the flour as you can with the mixer. Using a wooden spoon, stir in any remaining flour.

3. Divide dough in half. If necessary, cover and chill 1 to 2 hours.

4. On a lightly floured surface, roll half of the dough at a time to ⅛-inch thickness. Using a diamond-shaped cutter about 3 inches in length, cut out dough. Place on prepared cookie sheet. Using an hors d'oeuvre cutter, cut out and remove a smaller diamond shape from the centers of half of the cookies. Place whole cookies on one cookie sheet and cutout cookies on another cookie sheet because they may bake at different rates.

5. Bake in a 375° oven for 5 to 7 minutes or until edges begin to brown. Transfer cookies to a wire rack; cool. If desired, glaze the cookies with cutouts with Powdered Sugar Icing and sprinkle with nonpareils; let dry.

6. To serve, spread the bottoms of the whole cookies with about ½ teaspoon of the Bittersweet Chocolate Spread; place a cookie with a cutout, bottom side down, on chocolate spread. Makes about 64 (3-inch) cookie sandwiches.

Powdered Sugar Icing: In a small mixing bowl stir together 1 cup sifted powdered sugar, ¼ teaspoon vanilla, and enough milk (2 to 4 teaspoons) to make of spreading consistency.

Bittersweet Chocolate Spread: In a heavy small saucepan melt 6 ounces cut up bittersweet chocolate and 2 tablespoons butter over low heat, stirring constantly. Cool slightly.

Nutrition facts per cookie: 62 cal., 3 g total fat (2 g sat. fat), 9 mg chol., 32 mg sodium, 8 g carbo., 0 g fiber, 1 g pro.

ingredients

½ cup butter, softened

1 cup granulated sugar

1 teaspoon baking powder

1 teaspoon freshly grated nutmeg or ground nutmeg (optional)

¼ teaspoon baking soda

Dash salt

½ cup mascarpone cheese or dairy sour cream

1 egg

2½ cups all-purpose flour

1 recipe Powdered Sugar Icing (optional)

White nonpareils (optional)

1 recipe Bittersweet Chocolate Spread

honey and poppy seed hearts

ingredients

¾ cup butter, softened

⅔ cup sugar

3 tablespoons honey

2 teaspoons finely shredded
   lemon or orange peel

1 teaspoon baking powder

1 teaspoon ground
   cinnamon

¼ teaspoon baking soda

1 egg

2¼ cups all-purpose flour

1 egg white

1 tablespoon water

2 tablespoons poppy seed

The addition of honey to these cinnamon-spiced cookies gives them great flavor and a slightly soft texture.

Prep: 40 minutes   Chill: 2 hours   Bake: 8 to 10 minutes

1. Lightly grease a cookie sheet; set aside.

2. In a large mixing bowl beat butter with electric mixer on medium to high speed about 30 seconds. Add the sugar, honey, lemon or orange peel, baking powder, cinnamon, and baking soda. Beat until combined, scraping sides of bowl occasionally. Beat in the egg until combined. Beat in as much of the flour as you can with the mixer. Using a wooden spoon, stir in any remaining flour.

3. Divide dough in half. Cover and chill about 2 hours or until dough is easy to handle.

4. On a lightly floured surface, roll half of the dough at a time to ¼-inch thickness. Using a 2½- to 3-inch heart-shaped cookie cutter, cut out dough. Place 2 inches apart on prepared cookie sheet. To later be able to string cookies together with a ribbon (see photo, right), use a straw to make a hole in the center of each cookie.

5. In a small bowl beat egg white with water. Brush tops of the cookies with egg white mixture and sprinkle with poppy seed.

6. Bake in a 375° oven for 8 to 10 minutes or until edges are golden. Transfer cookies to a wire rack; cool. Makes about 36 (2½-inch) cookies.

Nutrition facts per cookie: 85 cal., 4 g total fat (2 g sat. fat), 16 mg chol., 61 mg sodium, 11 g carbo., 0 g fiber, 1 g pro.

These Honey and Poppy Seed Hearts strung on a ribbon will play the heartstrings of anyone with a sentimental side or sweet tooth. The cookie wreath can be given on a pretty plate or in a festive gift box. For decoration, tie individual cookies to a heart-shaped grapevine wreath with floral ribbons.

SHAPES OF THE SEASON

cranberry pockets

ingredients

- ½ cup butter, softened
- 1 cup granulated sugar
- ½ teaspoon baking powder
- ¼ teaspoon baking soda
- ¼ teaspoon ground nutmeg
- Dash salt
- ½ cup dairy sour cream
- 1 egg
- 2 teaspoons finely shredded orange peel
- ½ teaspoon vanilla
- 2⅔ cups all-purpose flour
- 1 recipe Cranberry-Port Filling
- 1 recipe Port Glaze
- 1 recipe Powdered Sugar Icing

A surprise awaits inside these pockets—a sweet-tart cranberry filling flavored with the richness of port wine.

Prep: 1 hour   Chill: 1 to 2 hours   Bake: 7 to 8 minutes

1. In a large bowl beat butter with electric mixer on medium speed for 30 seconds. Beat in granulated sugar, baking powder, soda, nutmeg, and salt. Beat in sour cream, egg, orange peel, and vanilla. Beat in as much flour as you can. Stir in remaining flour. Divide dough in half. Cover and chill for 1 to 2 hours or until easy to handle.

2. On a well-floured surface, roll half of the dough at a time to ⅛-inch thickness. Using a 3-inch round cookie cutter, cut out dough. Place cookies on an ungreased cookie sheet. Spoon about ½ teaspoon cooled Cranberry-Port Filling onto the center of each round. Fold in half. Seal edges together, pressing with tines of fork.

3. Bake in a 375° oven for 7 to 8 minutes or until edges are firm and bottoms are very lightly browned. Transfer cookies to a wire rack; cool. When cookies are cool, drizzle with Port Glaze and Powdered Sugar Icing. Makes about 42 cookies.

Cranberry-Port Filling: In a small saucepan combine ¾ cup dried cranberries, ⅓ cup port wine or cranberry-apple drink, and 2 tablespoons orange juice. Bring just to boiling; reduce heat. Simmer, uncovered, 5 to 10 minutes or until cranberries are tender and most of liquid is absorbed, stirring occasionally. Remove from heat; stir in 3 tablespoons granulated sugar. Cool slightly. Transfer mixture to a food processor or blender container. Cover and process or blend until cranberries are finely chopped. Cool completely.

Port Glaze: In a small bowl stir together 1 cup sifted powdered sugar and enough port wine or cranberry-apple drink (3 to 4 teaspoons) to make glaze of drizzling consistency. Tint with a small amount of red food coloring, if desired.

Powdered Sugar Icing: In a small mixing bowl stir together 1 cup sifted powdered sugar, ¼ teaspoon vanilla, and enough milk (3 to 4 teaspoons) to make icing of drizzling consistency.

Nutrition facts per cookie: 104 cal., 3 g total fat (2 g sat. fat), 12 mg chol., 41 mg sodium, 18 g carbo., 0 g fiber, 1 g pro.

Few scents and tastes so turn our minds to the holidays than those of the tart, vividly colored cranberry. As an inspiring gift for your favorite cook, fill a decorative metal baking tin with a few fresh cranberries and some Cranberry Pockets. Wrap the filled tin with a pretty kitchen towel.

pecan balls

ingredients

- 1 cup butter, softened
- ½ cup very fine granulated sugar
- ¼ teaspoon salt
- 2 teaspoons vanilla
- 2 cups all-purpose flour
- 1 cup finely chopped pecans
- Fine granulated sugar, colored fine sugar*, and/or powdered sugar

Countless cookie plates across the country would surely look incomplete without the presence of this holiday classic. This version is rolled in a mixture of tinted fine granulated and powdered sugars.

Prep: 35 minutes   Bake: 12 minutes

1. In a large mixing bowl beat butter with an electric mixer on medium to high speed for 30 seconds. Add the ½ cup granulated sugar and the salt. Beat until combined. Beat in vanilla. Beat in as much of the flour as you can with the mixer. Using a wooden spoon, stir in any remaining flour. Stir in pecans.

2. Shape slightly rounded teaspoons of dough into balls the size of large grapes. Place balls 1 inch apart on an ungreased cookie sheet.

3. Bake in a 350° oven about 12 minutes or until bottoms just begin to brown.

4. While cookies are still warm, roll them in a mixture of additional fine granulated sugar, colored fine sugar, and/or powdered sugar. Transfer cookies to a wire rack; cool. Makes about 72 cookies.

*Note: To make colored fine sugar, place ⅔ cup fine granulated sugar in a small bowl. Fill a ¼-teaspoon measure with water. Add 1 or 2 drops pink liquid food coloring to the water. Sprinkle colored water over sugar in bowl. Stir until combined and color is evenly distributed. Do not overmoisten or the sugar will begin to dissolve.

Nutrition facts per cookie: 52 cal., 4 g total fat (2 g sat. fat), 7 mg chol., 33 mg sodium, 5 g carbo., 0 g fiber, 0 g pro.

toasted pine nut wedges

Toasting pine nuts brings out their rich, buttery flavor in this simple, but sophisticated, shortbread cookie.

Prep: 25 minutes   Bake: 15 to 20 minutes

1. In a medium mixing bowl combine flour and brown sugar. Using a pastry blender, cut in butter until mixture resembles coarse crumbs. Stir in the finely chopped pine nuts. Add water, 1 teaspoon at a time, tossing with a fork, until moistened. Form mixture into a ball. Divide dough in half.

2. On a lightly floured surface, roll one portion of the dough at a time into a 6-inch circle. If desired, crimp edge with fingers. Cut each circle into 12 wedges.

Place wedges 1 inch apart on an ungreased cookie sheet. Place 3 pine nuts, side by side, at wide end of each wedge.

3. Bake in a 325° oven for 15 to 20 minutes or until bottoms just start to brown. Transfer cookies to a wire rack; cool. Makes 24 cookies.

Nutrition facts per cookie: 77 cal., 5 g total fat (3 g sat. fat), 10 mg chol., 40 mg sodium, 7 g carbo., 0 g fiber, 1 g pro.

ingredients

1¼ cups all-purpose flour
⅓ cup packed brown sugar
½ cup butter
¼ cup finely chopped
    toasted pine nuts
3 to 4 teaspoons water
2 to 3 tablespoons pine
    nuts

tasty, toasty nuts

Nuts are naturally rich and tasty right from the shell, but their flavor can be enhanced by a simple toasting step. Here's how to do it. Spread the nuts in a single layer in a shallow baking pan. Bake in a 350° oven for 5 to 10 minutes or until the nuts are light golden brown, watching them carefully and stirring once or twice so they don't burn.

   Nuts can be "toasted" in the microwave. Place nuts in a 2-cup measure. Cook, uncovered, on 100 percent power (high) until they are light golden brown, stirring after 2 minutes, then stirring every 30 seconds. Allow 2 to 3 minutes for ½ cup almonds or pecans, 2 to 3 minutes for 1 cup almonds, 3 to 4 minutes for 1 cup pecans, 3 to 4 minutes for ½ cup raw peanuts or walnuts, and 3½ to 5 minutes for 1 cup raw peanuts or walnuts. Allow nuts to cool on paper towels. Nuts will continue to toast as they stand.

Decorative topiaries of fresh lemons were all the rage in colonial America at Christmastime. Here, a topiary of Orange Snowballs wound with lemon and lime peel spirals makes a lovely, and edible, addition to your buffet table. For a heart- and hand-warming gift, wrap snowballs individually in plastic wrap and tuck them inside a pair of mittens.

orange snowballs

Sparkling with a dusting of orange-infused sugar, these melt-in-your-mouth cookies make a lovely addition to a gift box of Christmas treats.

Prep: 25 minutes   **Bake:** 15 minutes

1. In a large mixing bowl beat butter with an electric mixer on medium to high speed for 30 seconds. Add powdered sugar. Beat until combined, scraping sides of bowl occasionally. Beat in orange juice until combined. Beat in as much of the flour as you can with mixer. Using a wooden spoon, stir in the 1 tablespoon orange peel and remaining flour.

2. Shape dough into 1¼-inch balls. Place balls 2 inches apart on an ungreased cookie sheet.

3. Bake in a 325° oven for 15 minutes or until bottoms are lightly browned. Cool on cookie sheet for 5 minutes.

4. Meanwhile in a food processor or a blender container combine the ¾ cup granulated sugar and the 2 teaspoons orange peel. Cover and process or blend until mixture is combined. Stir in edible glitter, if desired. Roll the baked cookies, still slightly warm, in the sugar mixture. Transfer cookies to a wire rack; cool. Makes about 48 cookies.

Cookie Topiary: To form a tree shape, stack some of the balls using canned vanilla frosting to hold the layers together. Garnish with narrow strips of lime and lemon peel.

Nutrition facts per cookie: 76 cal., 4 g total fat (2 g sat. fat), 10 mg chol., 6 mg sodium, 10 g carbo., 0 g fiber, 1 g pro.

ingredients

- 1 cup butter, softened
- ¾ cup sifted powdered sugar
- 1 tablespoon finely shredded orange peel (set aside)
- 2 teaspoons finely shredded orange peel (set aside)
- 1 tablespoon orange juice
- 2⅔ cups all-purpose flour
- ¾ cup granulated sugar
- 1 teaspoon gold edible glitter (optional)

chocolate shortbread

ingredients

- 1½ cups all-purpose flour
- ⅓ cup unsweetened cocoa powder
- ¾ cup butter, softened
- ¾ cup sifted powdered sugar
- ½ teaspoon vanilla
- ½ teaspoon almond extract
- ⅛ teaspoon salt
- 12 almond slices

In the minds of true chocolate-lovers, there's only one way to improve upon classic, pure butter shortbread. This one's for them.

Prep: 15 minutes   Bake: 30 minutes

1. Lightly grease a 9-inch fluted tart pan with removable bottom or a cookie sheet; set aside.

2. In a medium mixing bowl combine flour and cocoa powder; set aside. In a large mixing bowl beat butter with an electric mixer on medium to high speed for 30 seconds. Add powdered sugar, vanilla, almond extract, and salt. Beat until combined, scraping sides of bowl occasionally. Add flour mixture and combine until mixture resembles fine crumbs and starts to cling. Form mixture into a ball and knead until smooth.

3. Pat dough evenly into prepared pan or pat to a 9-inch circle on the prepared cookie sheet. Using your fingers, scallop the edge, if desired. Score into 12 wedges and prick each wedge 3 times with fork tines, making sure to go all the way through the dough. Press an almond slice into each wedge about ½ inch from the edge.

4. Bake in a 325° oven about 30 minutes or until top looks dry. Cool in pan on a wire rack for 5 minutes. Remove sides of tart pan, if using. Cool completely on wire rack. Cut into wedges. Makes 12 cookies.

Nutrition facts per cookie: 196 cal., 13 g total fat (7 g sat. fat), 31 mg chol., 24 mg sodium, 19 g carbo., 1 g fiber, 2 g pro.

black and white twists

These sophisticated sweets have real eye and mouth appeal. They're easy to make, too. Mix them up and shape them one day; then chill them overnight and bake them the next.

Prep: 45 minutes   Chill: 2 to 24 hours   Bake: 12 to 15 minutes

1. In a large mixing bowl beat butter with an electric mixer on medium to high speed for 30 seconds. Add powdered sugar and salt; beat until combined, scraping sides of bowl occasionally. Beat in egg and vanilla until combined. Beat in as much of the flour as you can with the mixer. Using a wooden spoon, stir in remaining flour.

2. Divide dough in half. Add the melted chocolate and milk to half of the dough.* Using your hands, knead dough until well combined.

3. On a lightly floured surface, shape each dough half into a 12-inch-long log. Cut each log into 12 equal pieces.

4. Roll each dough piece into a 12-inch-long rope about ½ inch thick. Place a chocolate rope and a vanilla rope side by side; gently twist together 8 to 10 times. Press lightly to seal ends and transfer to

a cookie sheet. Repeat with remaining dough. Cover and chill for 2 to 24 hours or until firm.

5. Lightly grease a cookie sheet; set aside.

6. Cut each twisted log into 2½-inch-long pieces. Dip one end of each piece into beaten egg white, then into the chopped nuts. Place cookies about 2 inches apart on the prepared cookie sheet.

7. Bake in a 350° oven for 12 to 15 minutes or until vanilla dough is lightly golden. Transfer cookies to a wire rack; cool. Makes 48 cookies.

Nutrition facts per cookie: 131 cal., 8 g total fat (4 g sat. fat), 20 mg chol., 26 mg sodium, 14 g carbo., 1 g fiber, 2 g pro.

Note: If desired, add several drops of food coloring to the vanilla dough half.

ingredients

1½ cups butter, softened

2½ cups sifted powdered sugar

¼ teaspoon salt

1 egg

1 teaspoon vanilla

4¼ cups all-purpose flour

2 ounces unsweetened chocolate, melted and cooled

1 tablespoon milk

1 slightly beaten egg white

1 cup finely chopped hazelnuts (filberts) or pecans

chocolate reindeer

ingredients

- 1 cup butter, softened
- 1½ cups sugar
- ⅓ cup unsweetened cocoa powder
- 2 teaspoons cream of tartar
- 1 teaspoon baking soda
- ½ teaspoon salt
- 3 eggs
- 1 teaspoon vanilla
- 3¼ cups all-purpose flour
- 72 small pretzel twists
- 72 candy-coated milk chocolate pieces
- 36 small red gumdrops

Attention all homeroom parents! Bake these adorable reindeer for a holiday-time treat and you'll be the most popular person at school.

Prep: 40 minutes   Chill: 3 hours   Bake: 7 to 9 minutes

1. In a large mixing bowl beat butter with an electric mixer on medium to high speed for 30 seconds. Add sugar, cocoa powder, cream of tartar, baking soda, and salt. Beat until combined, scraping sides of bowl occasionally. Beat in eggs and vanilla until combined. Beat in as much of the flour as you can with the mixer. Using a wooden spoon, stir in remaining flour.

2. Divide dough into 6 equal portions. Wrap portions in waxed paper or plastic wrap. Chill for 3 hours or until dough is easy to handle.

3. On a lightly floured surface, roll each dough portion into a circle 6 inches in diameter. Using a knife, cut each circle into 6 wedges. Place wedges 2 inches apart on an ungreased cookie sheet.

4. For antlers, on each triangle lightly press a pretzel into the upper corners. Press in chocolate pieces for eyes. For a nose, press a red gumdrop into the dough triangle about ½ inch from the point.

5. Bake in a 375° oven for 7 to 9 minutes or until edges are firm. Do not overbake. Cool on cookie sheet for 1 minute. Transfer cookies to a wire rack; cool. Makes 36 cookies.

Nutrition facts per cookie: 191 cal., 6 g total fat (3 g sat. fat), 31 mg chol., 316 mg sodium, 30 g carbo., 0 g fiber, 3 g pro.

There's nothing like a herd of Chocolate Reindeer for making a pack of hungry children happy. For a children's Christmas party (or just for fun), mix different candies along with the cookies in a muffin tin. Add a "reindeer food" sign attached to a crafts stick to the muffin tin.

citrus pinwheels

ingredients

- 1 cup butter, softened
- 1 3-ounce package cream cheese, softened
- ½ cup sugar
- 2 teaspoons finely shredded orange peel
- 1 teaspoon finely shredded lemon peel
- ½ teaspoon finely shredded lime peel
- ½ teaspoon vanilla
- 2¼ cups all-purpose flour
- 1 recipe Egg Yolk Paint

An easy egg yolk "paint" lets you get the decorating done on these spritz-with-a-citrus-twist cookies before they go in the oven.

Prep: 1¼ hours   Bake: 12 to 14 minutes

1. In a large mixing bowl beat butter and cream cheese with an electric mixer on medium to high speed for 30 seconds. Add sugar, orange peel, lemon peel, lime peel, and vanilla. Beat until combined, scraping sides of bowl occasionally. Beat in as much of the flour as you can with the mixer. Using a wooden spoon, stir in any remaining flour.

2. Pack unchilled dough into a cookie press fitted with a pinwheel plate. Force dough through press onto an ungreased cookie sheet. Brush the top of each cookie with all three Egg Yolk Paint colors.

3. Bake in a 375° oven for 12 to 14 minutes or until edges of cookies are firm but not brown. Transfer cookies to a wire rack; cool. Makes about 48 cookies.

Egg Yolk Paint: To make green, yellow, and orange paints, in each of 3 small bowls combine 1 egg yolk and 1 teaspoon water. Add 1 or 2 drops of green food coloring to one bowl, 1 or 2 drops of yellow food coloring to the second bowl, and 1 drop of red food coloring plus 4 drops of yellow food coloring to the third bowl.

Nutrition facts per cookie: 71 cal., 5 g total fat (3 g sat. fat), 26 mg chol., 45 mg sodium, 6 g carbo., 0 g fiber, 1 g pro.

a shred of peel

Just a tiny bit of shredded lime, lemon, or orange peel delivers a burst of flavor to cookies. If a recipe calls for shredded citrus peel, use only the colored surface of the peel, not the bitter-tasting, spongy, white pith. Hand graters and zesters are convenient, but you can also use a vegetable peeler to remove layers of peel. Finely mince the peel with a sharp kitchen knife. Prepare extra peel to keep on hand; freeze it in a resealable plastic bag.

spicy molasses waffle squares

Just for fun—and their delicious flavor, too—these molasses-spice cookies are baked in a waffle iron. (No one will be the wiser if you eat them for breakfast.)

Prep: 20 minutes   Bake: 1 minute for 4 cookies

1. Lightly grease a waffle baker; preheat.

2. In a mixing bowl stir together the all-purpose flour, whole wheat flour, brown sugar, baking powder, salt, cinnamon, ginger, and cloves; set aside.

3. In another mixing bowl combine eggs, melted butter, and molasses. Add egg mixture all at once to dry mixture. Stir just until the mixture is moistened.

4. Drop a rounded teaspoon of batter 3 inches apart onto the grids of the prepared waffle baker. Close the lid. Bake for 1 minute or until cookies are golden brown. When done, use a fork to lift cookies off the waffle baker.

5. Transfer cookies to a wire rack; cool. Repeat with remaining batter. When cookies are cool, drizzle with Orange Glaze. Store up to 3 days in the refrigerator or freeze for longer storage. Makes about 28 cookies.

ingredients

⅔ cup all-purpose flour

½ cup whole wheat flour

½ cup packed brown sugar

½ teaspoon baking powder

¼ teaspoon salt

¼ teaspoon ground cinnamon

⅛ teaspoon ground ginger
   Dash ground cloves

2 slightly beaten eggs

¼ cup butter or margarine, melted

2 tablespoons molasses

1 recipe Orange Glaze

Orange Glaze: In a small mixing bowl stir together 1 cup sifted powdered sugar and ½ teaspoon finely shredded orange peel. Stir in enough orange juice (3 to 4 teaspoons) to make glaze of drizzling consistency.

Nutrition facts per cookie: 67 cal., 2 g total fat (1 g sat. fat), 20 mg chol., 48 mg sodium, 11 g carbo., 0 g fiber, 1 g pro.

For an enthusiastic baker, a gift of Santa Madeleines nestled in a madeleine pan (along with the recipe) is a welcome invitation to experiment. Or, decorate a cardboard box with old Christmas cards and fill it with a dozen sweet St. Nicks.

santa madeleines

These soft, cakelike little cookies from France are made sweeter still when formed into the cherry-cheeked likeness of the jolliest old elf of them all—Santa Claus.

Prep: 1¼ hours   Bake: 10 minutes

ingredients

¾ cup all-purpose flour

¼ teaspoon baking powder

1 egg

2 egg yolks

1 cup sifted powdered sugar

½ cup butter, melted
    and cooled

2 teaspoons finely shredded
    orange peel

2 teaspoons orange juice

½ teaspoon anise seed,
    crushed (optional)

1 recipe Decorator Frosting
    or 2 cans vanilla
    frosting

Red, blue, green, pink,
    and/or black paste food
    coloring

Small round candies
    (optional)

1. Grease and flour twenty-four 3-inch madeleine molds; set aside. Stir together flour and baking powder; set aside.

2. In a medium mixing bowl beat egg and egg yolks with an electric mixer on high speed 5 minutes or until thick and lemon colored. Add powdered sugar; beat on low speed until combined, then on high speed about 5 minutes more or until very thick and satiny. Beat in butter with an electric mixer on low speed. Add flour mixture, beating at low speed until combined. Stir in orange peel, orange juice, and, if using, anise seed. Carefully spoon batter into the prepared molds, filling each three-fourths full.

3. Bake in a 375° oven about 10 minutes or until edges are golden and tops spring back. Cool in molds on rack 1 minute. Loosen cookies with a knife. Invert cookies onto a rack and cool completely.

4. Divide frosting, leaving about half of it white; color one-third with red and/or pink food coloring and remaining with green, black, and/or blue food coloring.

5. To decorate, fill a decorating bag fitted with a small star tip with white frosting. Pipe on hat trim at an angle about a third of the way down from narrow end of cookie. Fill decorating bag fitted with a small star or plain tip with red or pink frosting; pipe on hat. With white frosting, pipe on mustache, beard, and pom-pom on hat. Fill decorating bag fitted with a small round tip with green, black, or blue frosting; pipe on eyes. Using red frosting, pipe on mouth. Pipe on other frosting decorations. (Or, use small round candies for eyes, nose, mouth, and cheeks, attaching them with frosting.) Wrap cookies tightly to store. Makes 24 cookies.

Decorator Frosting: Beat 1 cup shortening and 1½ teaspoons vanilla on medium speed for 30 seconds. Slowly add 2 cups sifted powdered sugar; beat well. Beat in 2 tablespoons milk. Gradually beat in 2½ cups sifted powdered sugar and enough milk to make piping consistency.

Nutrition facts per cookie: 220 cal., 13 g total fat (5 g sat. fat), 37 mg chol., 47 mg sodium, 26 g carbo., 0 g fiber, 1 g pro.

bear-on-the-mountain cookies

ingredients

- ½ cup butter, softened
- 1 cup sugar
- ¼ teaspoon baking powder
- ¼ teaspoon baking soda
- ¼ teaspoon salt
- 1 egg
- 1½ teaspoons vanilla
- ½ cup unsweetened cocoa powder
- 1½ cups all-purpose flour
- 54 milk chocolate kisses or milk chocolate kisses with stripes
- ½ cup canned vanilla frosting
- 54 chewy fruit bear snacks or holiday-shaped chewy fruit snacks

The littlest bakers in your house will be thrilled to help decorate these whimsical treats. (Be aware that some of the bears will miss the mountain entirely, ending up in a smiling mouth instead!)

Prep: 30 minutes   **Bake:** 9 minutes

1. In a large mixing bowl beat butter with an electric mixer on medium to high speed for 30 seconds. Add sugar, baking powder, baking soda, and salt. Beat until combined, scraping the sides of the bowl occasionally. Beat in egg and vanilla until combined. Beat in cocoa powder and as much of the flour as you can with the mixer. Using a wooden spoon, stir in any remaining flour.

2. Shape the dough into 1-inch balls. Place the balls of dough 2 inches apart on an ungreased cookie sheet.

3. Bake in a 350° oven about 9 minutes or until edges are firm. Immediately press a chocolate kiss into center of each cookie. Transfer cookies to a wire rack; cool.

4. When cookies are cool, spoon frosting into a heavy self-sealing plastic bag. Using scissors, snip the tip off one corner of the bag. Pipe a small amount of frosting onto the top of each kiss. Stand a bear atop each cookie. Makes about 54 cookies.

Nutrition facts per cookie: 88 cal., 4 g total fat (2 g sat. fat), 8 mg chol., 43 mg sodium, 13 g carbo., 0 g fiber, 1 g pro.

peppermint candy canes

Make these delightful "cookie canes" with either red- or green-tinted dough or combine the two colors in one cane.

Prep: 25 minutes   Chill: 30 to 60 minutes   Bake: 7 to 8 minutes

ingredients

⅓ cup butter, softened

⅓ cup shortening

¾ cup sugar

1 teaspoon baking powder

   Dash salt

1 egg

1 tablespoon milk

½ teaspoon vanilla

½ teaspoon peppermint
   extract

2 cups all-purpose flour

   Red or green paste
   food coloring

   Sugar (optional)

1. In a medium mixing bowl beat butter and shortening with an electric mixer on medium to high speed for 30 seconds. Add the ¾ cup sugar, the baking powder, and salt. Beat until combined, scraping sides of bowl occasionally. Beat in egg, milk, vanilla, and peppermint extract. Beat in as much of the flour as you can with the mixer. Using a wooden spoon, stir in any remaining flour.

2. Divide dough in half. Stir red or green paste food coloring into half of the dough. If necessary, cover and chill dough for 30 to 60 minutes or until dough is easy to handle.

3. Divide each half into 6 pieces. Roll each piece into a 12-inch-long rope. Lay ropes side by side on a lightly floured surface, alternating colors. With a rolling pin, roll assembled ropes into about a 14×9-inch rectangle that is ¼ inch thick. Using a pastry cutter, pizza wheel, or long sharp knife, cut the rectangle diagonally into ½-inch-wide strips. Cut strips into pieces about 5 to 7 inches long. (Press shorter strips together end to end to reach desired length.) Place on an ungreased cookie sheet. Curve one end of each piece to form a candy cane. If desired, sprinkle lightly with additional sugar.

4. Bake in a 375° oven for 7 to 8 minutes or until edges are firm and bottoms are very lightly browned Transfer cookies to a wire rack; cool. Makes about 36 cookies.

Nutrition facts per cookie: 74 cal., 4 g total fat (2 g sat. fat), 10 mg chol., 33 mg sodium, 9 g carbo., 0 g fiber, 1 g pro.

51

chocolate-mint sticks

ingredients

½ cup butter, softened

¼ cup shortening

½ cup packed brown sugar

2 teaspoons milk

½ teaspoon vanilla

¼ teaspoon salt

1¾ cups all-purpose flour

½ cup miniature semisweet chocolate pieces

1¼ cups white baking pieces

¼ cup sweetened condensed milk*

¼ teaspoon mint extract

2 or 3 drops red or green food coloring

2 teaspoons shortening

Few drops red or green food coloring (optional)

Though they may look like biscotti, these chocolate-dotted cookies with a creamy, mint-flavored white chocolate filling require no dipping to be soft and delectable.

Prep: 25 minutes Chill: 30 minutes Bake: 15 to 20 minutes

1. Lightly grease a cookie sheet; set aside.

2. In a large mixing bowl beat butter and the ¼ cup shortening with an electric mixer on medium to high speed for 30 seconds. Add brown sugar, milk, vanilla, and salt. Beat until combined, scraping sides of bowl occasionally. Beat in as much of the flour as you can with the mixer. Using a wooden spoon, stir in any remaining flour. Stir in chocolate pieces. If necessary, cover and chill dough for 30 minutes or until it is easy to handle.

3. Meanwhile, for filling, in a small saucepan combine ¾ cup of the white baking pieces and the sweetened condensed milk. Cook and stir over low heat until baking pieces melt. Remove from heat; cool slightly. Stir in mint extract and 2 or 3 drops of red or green food coloring.

4. Divide dough in half. On a lightly floured surface, roll one portion of dough into a 12×6-inch rectangle. Spread half of the filling lengthwise over half of

dough to within ½ inch of edges. Carefully fold dough rectangle in half to cover the filling; seal all edges. Repeat with remaining dough and filling. Transfer filled dough rectangles to prepared cookie sheet.

5. Bake in a 350° oven for 15 to 20 minutes or until edges are lightly browned. Cool on cookie sheet on a wire rack. Transfer to a cutting board. Cut crosswise into ¾-inch-wide strips.

6. In a heavy small saucepan combine the remaining ½ cup white baking pieces and 2 teaspoons shortening; heat over low heat until melted, stirring occasionally. Remove from heat. If desired, stir in a few drops of red or green food coloring. Drizzle over cookie strips. Makes about 30 cookies.

Note: Transfer the remaining sweetened condensed milk to a covered storage container and store in the refrigerator for up to 3 days.

Nutrition facts per cookie: 142 cal., 8 g total fat (4 g sat. fat), 12 mg chol., 61 mg sodium, 15 g carbo., 0 g fiber, 2 g pro.

Chocolate-Mint Sticks look very much at home presented in a frosted glass bowl. Or, line a cardboard pencil box (similar to a cigar box) with tissue paper and fill it with a neat row of these cookies. A frosted-glass holiday ornament with the recipient's name written in permanent marker makes a memorable gift tag.

cashew-filled sandwich cookies

ingredients

- ½ cup shortening
- ⅓ cup granulated sugar
- ⅓ cup packed brown sugar
- ½ teaspoon baking powder
- ¼ teaspoon baking soda
- ⅛ teaspoon salt
- 1 egg
- 1 teaspoon vanilla
- 1½ cups all-purpose flour
- ¾ cup quick-cooking rolled oats
- 1 recipe Cashew-Butter Filling or ½ cup chocolate-hazelnut spread
- 1 recipe Chocolate Glaze (optional)
- Finely chopped cashews (optional)

Look for the filling's cashew butter at a natural foods store. Chocolate-hazelnut spread, available at most grocery stores, can be substituted, if you like.

Prep: 1¼ hours   Bake: 5 to 7 minutes

1. In bowl beat shortening on medium to high speed 30 seconds. Add sugars, baking powder, baking soda, and salt. Beat until combined. Beat in egg and vanilla until combined. Beat in as much flour as you can. Stir in any remaining flour and oats. Shape dough into ½-inch balls. Place balls 2 inches apart on an ungreased cookie sheet. Flatten balls into 1-inch circles.

2. Bake in a 375° oven 5 to 7 minutes or until edges are firm and bottoms are lightly browned. Transfer to rack; cool.

3. Spread bottom of half the cookies with a scant ½ teaspoon Cashew-Butter Filling. Place another cookie, top side up, on filling. If desired, spoon a little glaze on top and sprinkle nuts over glaze. Let stand until set. Cover and store in refrigerator up to 3 days or freeze for longer storage. Makes about 78 sandwich cookies.

Cashew-Butter Filling: In bowl beat ⅓ cup cashew butter and 2 tablespoons softened butter until fluffy. Slowly beat in ½ cup sifted powdered sugar and

1 tablespoon milk. Beat in additional milk, if needed, for spreading consistency.

Chocolate Glaze: In a heavy small saucepan melt 1 cup semisweet chocolate pieces and 1 tablespoon shortening over low heat, stirring mixture frequently.

Nutrition facts per cookie: 35 cal., 2 g total fat (1 g sat. fat), 4 mg chol., 14 mg sodium, 4 g carbo., 0 g fiber, 0 g pro.

santa's lists

Santa (or someone with more permanent residence at your house) may make these lists, but he won't have a chance to check them twice if there are hungry elves around!

Prep: 30 minutes   **Bake:** 5 to 6 minutes

1. In a large mixing bowl beat butter and almond paste with an electric mixer on medium to high speed for 30 seconds. Add granulated sugar and baking powder. Beat until combined, scraping sides of bowl occasionally. Beat in egg and orange peel until combined. Beat in as much of the flour as you can with the mixer. Using a wooden spoon, stir in remaining flour.

2. Pack unchilled dough into a cookie press fitted with a ribbon plate. Force dough through press onto an ungreased cookie sheet in the shape of a swirled scroll (see photo), cutting into desired lengths.

3. Bake in a 375° oven for 5 to 6 minutes or until edges of cookies are firm but not brown. Transfer cookies to a wire rack; cool. When cooled, if desired, brush cookies with powdered food coloring and use Decorating Icing in a decorating bag with a writing tip to write names on cookies. Makes about 80 cookies.

Decorating Icing: In a small mixing bowl combine 3 cups sifted powdered sugar and enough milk (about 3 to 5 tablespoons) to make an icing of piping consistency. If desired, stir in a few drops of food coloring.

Nutrition facts per cookie: 53 cal., 3 g total fat (1 g sat. fat), 9 mg chol., 29 mg sodium, 6 g carbo., 0 g fiber, 1 g pro.

ingredients

1   cup butter, softened
½   of an 8-ounce can (½ cup) almond paste
1   cup granulated sugar
1   teaspoon baking powder
1   egg
1   tablespoon finely shredded orange peel
3   cups all-purpose flour
    Powdered food coloring
1   recipe Decorating Icing (optional)

Embellish miniature metal pails
reminiscent of sap buckets with
tiny bits of holiday trim to make
cute carriers for a sampling of
these maple-flavored cookies.
As a go-along gift, package
Maple Log Cabins and Trees
with a rustic picture frame
made of sticks.

maple log cabins and trees

Create the coziness of a cabin in the middle of the Vermont woods with a warm fire, a cup of coffee, and, of course, these delicious cabin- and tree-shaped cookies.

Prep: 1 hour   Chill: 1 to 2 hours   Bake: 8 to 10 minutes

ingredients

1½ cups butter, softened

1½ cups packed brown sugar

 2 eggs

¼ cup maple-flavored syrup

 4 cups all-purpose flour

 1 cup finely chopped
       toasted pecans

 1 egg white

 1 tablespoon water

 1 recipe Maple Icing
       White or colored
          nonpareils (optional)

1. In bowl beat butter on medium to high speed 30 seconds. Add brown sugar. Beat until combined. Beat in eggs and syrup until combined. Beat in as much of the flour as you can. Using a wooden spoon, stir in pecans and any remaining flour. Divide dough in half. Cover and chill for 1 to 2 hours. Divide each half of the dough into 12 portions. Roll each portion into a 10-inch-long rope.

2. For a cabin, cut a rope into five 2-inch-long logs. To assemble, place 3 logs horizontally on an ungreased cookie sheet; press them together slightly to form the cabin. Place the remaining 2 logs in an inverted V shape above the cabin; press ends against cabin corners slightly to form the roof. Brush with a mixture of egg white and water.

3. For a tree, cut a rope into 6 pieces: one 3-inch piece, one 2½-inch, one 2-inch, two 1-inch, and one ½-inch. To assemble, place the 3-inch piece horizontally on an ungreased cookie sheet; add the 2½-inch piece, then the 2-inch, a 1-inch, and finally the ½-inch piece; press them together slightly to form the tree. Place the remaining 1-inch piece vertically below the tree; press in place slightly to form the trunk. Brush with a mixture of egg white and water.

4. Bake in a 375° oven for 8 to 10 minutes or until edges are lightly browned. Cool on cookie sheet 1 minute. Transfer cookies to rack; cool. Using a decorating bag fitted with a plain tip or a plastic bag with corner snipped off, decorate each cookie as desired with Maple Icing. If desired, while icing is still wet, sprinkle with nonpareils. Makes 24 cabins or trees.

Maple Icing: In bowl beat 2 tablespoons butter for 30 seconds. Gradually beat in ¾ cup sifted powdered sugar. Beat in 3 tablespoons maple-flavored syrup. Gradually beat in enough sifted powdered sugar (½ to ¾ cup) for piping consistency. If desired, tint with food coloring.

Nutrition facts per cookie: 291 cal., 16 g total fat (8 g sat. fat), 51 mg chol., 137 mg sodium, 35 g carbo., 1 g fiber, 3 g pro.

orange curd tarts

Imbue your dessert table with the elegance of an English Christmas with these tiny tarts filled with homemade orange curd.

Prep: 45 minutes   Bake: 20 to 25 minutes

ingredients

1 package piecrust mix
    (for 2 crusts)

¼ cup finely chopped pecans

⅓ cup cold water

1 cup sugar

2 teaspoons cornstarch

1 tablespoon finely
    shredded orange
    peel (set aside)

⅓ cup orange juice

2 tablespoons butter, cut up

3 beaten eggs

½ cup coarsely chopped
    pecans (optional)

   Small orange peel
    curls (optional)

1. Lightly grease thirty-two 1¾-inch muffin pans; set aside.

2. In a small mixing bowl stir together piecrust mix and the ¼ cup finely chopped pecans. Add cold water and stir until moistened. Divide dough in half.

3. On a lightly floured surface, roll half of the dough at a time into a 10½-inch square; trim to a 10-inch square. Cut each square into sixteen 2½-inch squares. Fit squares into muffin cups, pleating sides and leaving corners standing up slightly.

4. For filling, in a medium saucepan combine sugar and cornstarch. Add orange juice and butter. Cook and stir over medium heat until thickened and bubbly. Cook and stir 2 minutes more. Stir about half of the juice mixture into beaten

eggs. Return juice-egg mixture to saucepan. Remove from heat. Stir in finely shredded orange peel.

5. Spoon about 2 teaspoons orange mixture into each dough-lined muffin cup. If desired, top with a few coarsely chopped pecans.

6. Bake in a 350° oven for 20 to 25 minutes or until filling is set and crust is lightly browned. Cool in pans on wire rack for 20 minutes. Carefully remove from pans and transfer to wire rack; cool. If desired, garnish tops with a small orange peel curl just before serving. Makes 32 cookies.

Nutrition facts per cookie: 96 cal., 5 g total fat (1 g sat. fat), 22 mg chol., 81 mg sodium, 12 g carbo., 0 g fiber, 1 g pro.

58

toy cookies

For kids, the only thing better than getting their heart's desire in a stocking is getting it with a glass of milk before bed. Shape these cookies into any kind of toy you (or your child) can imagine.

Prep: 2 hours   Chill: 2 to 24 hours   Bake: 18 to 20 minutes

1. In bowl beat butter and shortening for 30 seconds. Add sugar, baking powder, and salt. Beat until combined. Beat in eggs and vanilla until combined. Beat in as much of the flour as you can. Stir in any remaining flour (dough should be stiff).

2. Divide dough into portions, one for each color to be used. Knead food coloring into each portion, adding it slowly until desired color is obtained. Cover and chill for 2 to 24 hours. Shape dough into toy shapes (as described or others). Place cookies 2 inches apart on an ungreased cookie sheet.

3. Bake in a 300° oven for 18 to 20 minutes or until edges are firm. Carefully transfer cookies to a wire rack; cool. Makes about 40 cookies.

Car/bus: Flatten a 1½-inch piece of dough into a triangle with 2-inch sides. Round the corners and gently press the sides to make a vehicle body. Add two ½-inch balls for wheels. If desired, flatten pieces of dough for windows, headlights, bumpers, and people inside (see photo).

Tractor: For large wheel, flatten a 1¼ inch ball of dough. For tractor body, flatten a 1-inch ball of dough; attach to large wheel. For small wheel, flatten a ¾-inch ball of dough. For cab, shape a ¾-inch ball of dough; attach to large wheel and tractor body. For engine and hub cab, shape ½-inch balls of dough.

Teddy Bear: For body, flatten a 1½-inch ball of dough to about 1½ inches across. For head, flatten a ¾-inch ball of dough to about 1 inch across; press in place. Make six ⅜-inch balls; press in place for ears, arms, and legs. Add small dots of dough for eyes, nose, and mouth.

Boat: For the base, flatten a 1½-inch ball of dough into an oval to about 2½ inches across; curve ends up slightly. For a mast, attach a 2-inch-long piece of a different color in the center top of the base. For sails, flatten 2 triangles of dough and attach to mast.

Nutrition facts per cookie: 136 cal., 7 g total fat (3 g sat. fat), 20 mg chol., 79 mg sodium, 16 g carbo., 0 g fiber, 2 g pro.

ingredients

- ¾ cup butter, softened
- ⅔ cup butter-flavor or regular shortening
- 1½ cups sugar
- 1 tablespoon baking powder
- ¼ teaspoon salt
- 2 eggs
- 2 teaspoons vanilla
- 4 cups all-purpose flour
  Paste or liquid food coloring

chocolate-almond bonbons

ingredients

1 12-ounce package
   (2 cups) semisweet
   chocolate pieces

¼ cup butter

1 14-ounce can (1¼ cups)
   sweetened condensed
   milk

1 teaspoon vanilla

2 cups all-purpose flour

1 8-ounce can almond
   paste (made without
   syrup or glucose)

1 recipe Almond Glaze

1 recipe Chocolate Glaze
   (optional)

  Assorted small candies
   (optional)

  Purchased decorator icing
   (optional)

Half cookie, half confection, these marzipan-filled sweets are at home on a cookie tray or in a candy dish. Serve them in miniature paper bake cups to emphasize the "bonbon" look.

Prep: 1 hour   **Bake:** 6 to 8 minutes

1. In a medium saucepan combine chocolate pieces and butter. Cook and stir over low heat until melted and smooth. Stir in sweetened condensed milk and vanilla. Stir in flour until well combined.

2. Shape a slightly rounded teaspoon of dough around ½ teaspoon of almond paste. Repeat with remaining dough and almond paste. Place on an ungreased cookie sheet.

3. Bake in a 350° oven for 6 to 8 minutes or until chocolate is soft and shiny (do not overbake). Transfer cookies to a wire rack; cool. Drizzle or spoon Almond Glaze over cookies. If desired, substitute Chocolate Glaze for the Almond Glaze and decorate with small candies and decorator icing. Makes about 90 cookies.

Almond Glaze: In a small mixing bowl stir together 1 cup sifted powdered sugar, ½ teaspoon almond extract, and enough milk (about 1 to 2 tablespoons) to make glaze of drizzling consistency. If desired, tint with a few drops of red food coloring.

Chocolate Glaze: In a small mixing bowl stir together ½ cup sifted powdered sugar, 2 tablespoons unsweetened cocoa powder, and enough milk (about 2 to 3 teaspoons) to make of drizzling consistency.

Nutrition facts per cookie: 61 cal., 3 g total fat (1 g sat. fat), 3 mg chol., 11 mg sodium, 9 g carbo., 0 g fiber, 1 g pro.

Pretty and feminine Chocolate-Almond Bonbons could not be packaged more perfectly for giving than in a satin-covered box. Add a satin rope tie with tassel ends or a big, beautiful, faux-pearl encrusted bow. Write the lucky recipient's name on the ribbon using a paint pen.

cornmeal shortbread

ingredients

1 cup all-purpose flour

½ cup yellow cornmeal

¾ cup butter, softened

⅔ cup sifted powdered
    sugar

¾ teaspoon vanilla

Dash salt

Powdered sugar
    (optional)

Cornmeal adds a golden hue and delicate crunch to this tender, buttery shortbread. If you use a decorative shortbread mold, the dusting of powdered sugar after baking is a nice—though not necessary—touch.

Prep: 20 minutes   Bake: 25 to 30 minutes

1. Lightly grease a 9-inch fluted tart pan with removable bottom. Or, lightly grease and flour a 9-inch shortbread mold; set aside.

2. In a medium bowl stir together flour and cornmeal; set aside.

3. In a medium mixing bowl beat butter, powdered sugar, vanilla, and salt with an electric mixer on medium to high speed until well combined. Add flour mixture. Beat until combined, scraping sides of bowl occasionally.

4. Using your fingertips, pat dough evenly into prepared pan; score into 12 wedges. Prick each wedge 3 times with tines of a fork, making sure to go all the way through. If using a shortbread mold, do not prick the dough.

5. Bake in a 325° oven for 25 to 30 minutes or until top looks dry and edges are slightly browned. Cool in pan or mold on a wire rack for 5 minutes. Carefully remove ring from tart pan or shortbread from mold; cut shortbread into wedges. Transfer wedges to wire rack; cool. If desired, sift additional powdered sugar over the tops before serving. Makes 12 cookies.

Nutrition facts per cookie: 178 cal., 12 g total fat (7 g sat. fat), 31 mg chol., 128 mg sodium, 17 g carbo., 1 g fiber, 2 g pro.

eggnog thumbprints

Tender, walnut-encrusted, nutmeg-infused butter cookies serve as delicious vessels for a creamy, rum-flavored filling. Pipe the filling in just before serving so it holds its shape.

Prep: 45 minutes   Chill: 1 hour   Bake: 10 to 12 minutes

1. Lightly grease a cookie sheet; set aside.

2. In a large mixing bowl beat butter with an electric mixer on medium to high speed for 30 seconds. Add granulated sugar and the ⅛ teaspoon nutmeg. Beat until combined, scraping sides of bowl occasionally. Beat in egg yolks and vanilla. Beat in as much of the flour as you can with the mixer. Using a wooden spoon, stir in any remaining flour.

3. If necessary, cover and chill about 1 hour or until dough is easy to handle.

4. Shape dough into 1-inch balls. Roll balls in egg whites, then in chopped walnuts to coat. Place balls about 1 inch apart on prepared cookie sheet. Press your thumb into the center of each ball.

5. Bake in a 375° oven for 10 to 12 minutes or until edges are lightly browned. Transfer cookies to a wire rack; cool. When cookies are cool, pipe or spoon about ½ teaspoon Rum Filling into the center of each. Sprinkle with additional nutmeg. Makes about 40 cookies.

Rum Filling: In a small mixing bowl beat ¼ cup butter until softened. Add 1 cup sifted powdered sugar and beat until fluffy. Beat in 1 teaspoon rum or ¼ teaspoon rum extract and enough milk (1 to 2 teaspoons) to make a filling of spreading consistency.

Nutrition facts per cookie: 96 cal., 6 g total fat (3 g sat. fat), 22 mg chol., 46 mg sodium, 9 g carbo., 0 g fiber, 1 g pro.

ingredients

⅔ cup butter, softened

½ cup granulated sugar

⅛ teaspoon ground nutmeg

2 egg yolks

1 teaspoon vanilla

1½ cups all-purpose flour

2 slightly beaten egg whites

1 cup finely chopped walnuts

1 recipe Rum Filling
    Ground nutmeg

Like make-believe, brilliantly colored Marbled Magic Wands bring pure delight to a child's holiday. For party time, create a centerpiece of clear glasses (a variety of sizes adds interest) partially filled with colored sugars and these cookies. Wrap some of the glasses in brightly colored polka-dot ribbons. Children and adults alike will marvel at the color and sparkle.

marbled magic wands

Dub yourself the royal baker and the kids your loyal helpers with these treats. A little kitchen magic—food coloring, a cookie press, and colored sugars and candies—gives them the wow! factor kids love.

Prep: 40 minutes   **Bake:** 10 minutes

1. In a large mixing bowl beat butter with an electric mixer on medium to high speed for 30 seconds. Add granulated sugar and baking powder. Beat until combined, scraping sides of bowl occasionally. Beat in egg and vanilla. Beat in as much of the flour as you can with the mixer. Using a wooden spoon, stir in remaining flour.

2. Divide dough in half. Tint half of the dough as desired with paste food coloring. Leave the remaining half of dough plain or tint with another color.

3. Pack unchilled dough in both colors into a cookie press fitted with a large star plate, keeping the doughs separate by placing them side by side in the press. Force dough through press onto an ungreased cookie sheet to form wands about 5 inches long.

4. Bake in a 375° oven about 10 minutes or until edges are firm but not brown. Cool on cookie sheet for 1 minute. Transfer cookies to a wire rack; cool.

5. In a heavy small saucepan heat and stir white baking pieces and shortening over low heat until melted.

6. Dip an end of each cookie into melted white baking pieces, allowing excess to drip off. Sprinkle with colored sugar or multicolored candies. Place on waxed paper and allow coating to set. Makes about 36 cookies.

Nutrition facts per cookie: 153 cal., 8 g total fat (5 g sat. fat), 22 mg chol., 71 mg sodium, 18 g carbo., 0 g fiber, 2 g pro.

ingredients

 1 cup butter, softened
 1 cup granulated sugar
 1 teaspoon baking powder
 1 egg
 2 teaspoons vanilla
3½ cups all-purpose flour
    Paste food coloring
1½ cups white baking pieces
 1 tablespoon butter-flavor
    or regular shortening
    Colored sugars or small
    multicolored
    decorative candies

ginger crinkles

ingredients

- ¾ cup butter, softened
- 1 cup granulated sugar
- 1 teaspoon baking powder
- 1 teaspoon baking soda
- 2 teaspoons grated fresh ginger*
- ½ teaspoon ground cinnamon
- ½ teaspoon ground cloves
- ¼ teaspoon salt
- 1 egg
- ¼ cup molasses
- 2⅔ cups all-purpose flour
- ½ cup pearl or coarse sugar
- ¼ cup finely chopped crystallized ginger (optional)

A double dose of ginger—fresh and candied—fills the house with the scents of the season as these cookies bake.

Prep: 35 minutes   **Bake:** 8 to 10 minutes

1. In a large mixing bowl beat butter with an electric mixer on medium to high speed for 30 seconds. Add granulated sugar, baking powder, baking soda, fresh ginger, cinnamon, cloves, and salt. Beat until combined, scraping sides of bowl occasionally. Beat in egg and molasses. Beat in as much of the flour as you can with the mixer. Using a wooden spoon, stir in any remaining flour.

2. Shape dough into 1-inch balls. In a small bowl combine the pearl or coarse sugar and, if using, crystallized ginger. Roll balls in sugar mixture to coat. Place balls 2 inches apart on an ungreased cookie sheet.

3. Bake in a 375° oven for 8 to 10 minutes or until edges are set and tops are crackled. Cool on cookie sheet for 1 minute. Transfer cookies to a wire rack and let cool. Makes 48 cookies.

__Note:__ If crystallized ginger is omitted from the sugar mixture, use 1 tablespoon grated fresh ginger in the dough.

Nutrition facts per cookie: 78 cal., 3 g total fat (2 g sat. fat), 12 mg chol., 76 mg sodium, 12 g carbo., 0 g fiber, 1 g pro.

elf hats

To give these meringue elf-toppers their jocular colored pom-pom, pipe on a bit of tinted icing after baking.

Prep: 25 minutes   **Bake:** 15 minutes

1. In a medium mixing bowl allow egg whites to stand at room temperature for 30 minutes. Meanwhile, grease a cookie sheet; set aside.

2. Add vanilla, cream of tartar, and food coloring to the egg whites. Beat with an electric mixer on medium speed until soft peaks form (tips curl). Gradually add sugar, 1 tablespoon at a time, beating about 5 minutes on high speed until stiff peaks form (tips stand straight).

3. Spoon meringue into pastry bag fitted with ½-inch round tip. Pipe small 1-inch-high mounds that end in an angled tip about 1 inch apart on prepared sheet.

4. Bake in a 300° oven about 15 minutes or until edges are very lightly browned. Transfer cookies to a wire rack; cool.

5. When cookies are cool, dip bottoms into melted chocolate, then into chopped walnuts. Set on waxed paper until chocolate is firm. If desired, add a dot of colored icing to each tip. Makes about 48 cookies.

Nutrition facts per cookie: 41 cal., 2 g total fat (1 g sat. fat), 0 mg chol., 3 mg sodium, 5 g carbo., 0 g fiber, 1 g pro.

ingredients

- 2 egg whites
- ½ teaspoon vanilla
- ⅛ teaspoon cream of tartar
  Few drops green or red food coloring
- ⅔ cup sugar
- 6 ounces bittersweet chocolate or semisweet chocolate, melted
- ¾ cup finely chopped walnuts
  Purchased decorator icing (optional)

dazzling dips and drizzles

Dress up cookies with rich chocolate drips and drizzles, a snowlike coating of melted white baking bar, or a splash of tinted candy coating.

   To dip, gently stick half or all of a cooled cookie in melted chocolate; then remove excess with a small spatula or by pulling the cookie across the edge of the bowl.

   To drizzle, place cookies on a wire rack over waxed paper. Dip a fork into melted chocolate, letting the first clumpy drip land in the pan; then pass the fork over the cookies, letting the chocolate drizzle off. For added color, buy tinted candy coating. Or, tint melted white baking bar or candy coating with paste food coloring.

christmas flowers

ingredients

- ¾ cup butter, softened
- ⅔ cup shortening
- 1½ cups sugar
- 1 tablespoon baking powder
- ¼ teaspoon salt
- 2 eggs
- 1 teaspoon vanilla
- 4 cups all-purpose flour
- Paste or liquid food coloring

Despite being in the middle of winter, Christmas tradition is rife with references to flowers. Create cookies that look like poinsettias, complete with green leaves.

Prep: 40 minutes   **Chill:** 2 to 24 hours   **Bake:** 15 minutes

1. In a large mixing bowl beat butter and shortening with an electric mixer on medium to high speed for 30 seconds. Add sugar, baking powder, and salt. Beat until combined, scraping sides of bowl occasionally. Beat in eggs and vanilla until combined. Beat in as much of the flour as you can with the mixer. Using a wooden spoon, stir in any remaining flour (dough should be stiff).

2. Cover and chill dough at least 2 hours or overnight until dough is easy to handle.

3. Divide dough into portions, one for each color that you want to use. Knead food coloring into each portion, adding it slowly until the desired color is reached (colors lighten slightly when dough is baked). If desired, lightly knead two colors together for dough with a marbled appearance.

4. Break off small pieces of different colors of dough and form into flower shapes as shown in photo. (As a guideline, use about ½ teaspoon dough for each petal or leaf.) Place 2 inches apart on an ungreased cookie sheet. If desired, lightly mark lines in the dough to resemble veins in leaves.

5. Bake in a 300° oven for 15 minutes or until edges are firm and cookies look set but bottoms are not brown. Transfer cookies to a wire rack; cool. Makes about 24 cookies.

Nutrition facts per cookie: 226 cal., 12 g total fat (5 g sat. fat), 33 mg chol., 131 mg sodium, 27 g carbo., 1 g fiber, 3 g pro.

Almost too pretty to eat, Christmas Flowers in the shape and hues of holiday poinsettias are at home served in a small wooden box lined with parchment. To give as a party favor or gift, place a single flower cookie in a cellophane corsage bag and secure the top with a holiday pin.

yule logs

ingredients

- 1 cup butter, softened
- ¾ cup granulated sugar
- ¼ cup packed brown sugar
- ½ teaspoon ground nutmeg
- ½ teaspoon ground ginger
- 1 egg
- 1 tablespoon dark rum
- 1 teaspoon vanilla
- 3 cups all-purpose flour
- 1 recipe Browned Butter Frosting
- Petal dust, powdered food coloring, or ground nutmeg
- Purchased decorator icing (optional)

Put another log on the fire and bring out a fresh pot of coffee and a plate of these spiced cookies to inspire convivial conversation deep into the night. (Your favorite chocolate frosting will work on these, too.)

Prep: 1 hour   **Chill:** 30 minutes   **Bake:** 12 minutes

1. In a large mixing bowl beat butter with an electric mixer on medium to high speed about 30 seconds. Add granulated sugar, brown sugar, nutmeg, and ginger. Beat until combined, scraping sides of bowl occasionally. Beat in egg, rum, and vanilla. Beat in as much of the flour as you can with the mixer. Using a wooden spoon, stir in any remaining flour.

2. Divide dough into 6 pieces. Wrap and chill about 30 minutes or until easy to handle.

3. On a lightly floured surface, shape each piece into a rope ½ inch thick. Cut ropes into 3-inch-long logs. Place logs 2 inches apart on an ungreased cookie sheet.

4. Bake in a 350° oven about 12 minutes or until lightly browned. Transfer cookies to a wire rack; cool.

5. Spread Browned Butter Frosting over each cookie. Run a fork through the frosting so it resembles bark. Sprinkle lightly with petal dust, powdered food coloring, or ground nutmeg. If desired, add holly and berries of frosting. Makes about 48 cookies.

Browned Butter Frosting: In a small saucepan heat ½ cup butter over low heat until melted. Continue heating until butter turns a delicate brown. Remove from heat; pour into a medium mixing bowl. Add 5 cups sifted powdered sugar, ¼ cup milk, and 2 teaspoons vanilla. Beat with an electric mixer on low speed until combined. Beat on medium to high speed, adding additional milk (1 to 2 tablespoons), if necessary, to make frosting of spreading consistency.

Nutrition facts per cookie: 136 cal., 6 g total fat (4 g sat. fat), 20 mg chol., 61 mg sodium, 20 g carbo., 0 g fiber, 1 g pro.

coffee bean cookies

Paired with a pound of real coffee beans from your favorite gourmet java shop, these coffee-bean-shaped cookies made with cream cheese make a perfect gift for the true coffee-lover on your list.

Prep: 20 minutes **Chill:** 1 hour **Bake:** 9 to 11 minutes

1. Combine the coffee crystals and milk. Stir until the coffee crystals are dissolved; set aside.

2. Meanwhile, in a large mixing bowl beat butter and cream cheese with an electric mixer on medium to high speed for 30 seconds. Add brown sugar, vanilla, and milk-coffee mixture. Beat until mixture is combined, scraping sides of bowl occasionally. Beat in as much of the flour as you can with the mixer. Using a wooden spoon, stir in any remaining flour.

3. Cover and chill about 1 hour or until dough is easy to handle.

4. Shape dough into 1-inch balls. Shape each ball into an oval. Press the thin edge of a wooden spoon (or a chopstick) lengthwise into the top of each oval so they resemble coffee beans. Place 1 inch apart on an ungreased cookie sheet.

5. Bake in a 350° oven for 9 to 11 minutes or until edges are firm and bottoms are lightly browned. Transfer cookies to a wire rack; cool. Makes about 48 cookies.

Nutrition facts per cookie: 60 cal., 4 g total fat (2 g sat. fat), 10 mg chol., 36 mg sodium, 6 g carbo., 0 g fiber, 1 g pro.

ingredients

- 2 teaspoons instant coffee crystals
- 2 tablespoons milk
- ¾ cup butter, softened
- 1 3-ounce package cream cheese, softened
- ¾ cup packed brown sugar
- 1 teaspoon vanilla
- 2 cups all-purpose flour

SLICES OF DELIGHT

orange-chocolate rounds

ingredients

- 1 cup butter, softened
- 1½ cups sugar
- 1½ teaspoons baking powder
- ¼ teaspoon salt
- 1 egg
- 1 teaspoon vanilla
- 2½ cups all-purpose flour
- 2 teaspoons finely shredded orange peel
- 2 ounces unsweetened chocolate, melted and cooled slightly

Despite their sophisticated look, these fetching checkerboards are easy to make and shape. And with their highly appealing combination of chocolate and orange, they taste terrific, too.

Prep: 30 minutes   Chill: 3½ hours   Bake: 7 to 9 minutes

1. In a large mixing bowl beat butter with an electric mixer on medium to high speed for 30 seconds. Add sugar, baking powder, and salt. Beat until combined, scraping sides of bowl occasionally. Beat in egg and vanilla until combined. Beat in as much of the flour as you can with the mixer. Using a wooden spoon, stir in any remaining flour.

2. Divide dough in half. Stir orange peel into one dough half; stir melted chocolate into the other dough half. If necessary, cover and chill about 1 hour or until dough is easy to handle.

3. Shape each half of dough into a 10-inch-long roll. Wrap each roll in plastic wrap or waxed paper. Chill for 2 hours or until firm.

4. Cut each chilled roll lengthwise into quarters; reassemble rolls, alternating chocolate and orange quarters. Wrap and chill for 30 minutes more or until firm.

5. Using a sharp knife, cut dough into ¼-inch-thick slices. Place slices 1 inch apart on an ungreased cookie sheet.

6. Bake in a 375° oven for 7 to 9 minutes or until edges are firm and bottoms are lightly browned. Transfer cookies to a wire rack; cool. Makes about 60 cookies.

Nutrition facts per cookie: 70 cal., 4 g total fat (2 g sat. fat), 12 mg chol., 50 mg sodium, 9 g carbo., 0 g fiber, 1 g pro.

Dynamic Orange-Chocolate Rounds look terrific stacked in plain white porcelain boxes and tied with red-rimmed ribbon. If you're sending cheer to a faraway friend, wrap a stack of cookies in plastic wrap, top it off with a checkered bow, and seal it in a mailing tube.

cranberry-orange pinwheels

Here's a new spin on the pinwheel: Fresh cranberries give these delightfully different cookies (they're pleasingly soft rather than crisp, like most pinwheels) a refreshingly tangy taste and bright color.

Prep: 25 minutes   Chill: 5 to 24 hours   Bake: 8 to 10 minutes

ingredients

1	cup cranberries
1	cup pecans
¼	cup packed brown sugar
1	cup butter, softened
1½	cups granulated sugar
½	teaspoon baking powder
½	teaspoon salt
2	eggs
2	teaspoons finely shredded orange peel
3	cups all-purpose flour

1. For filling, in a blender container or food processor bowl, combine cranberries, pecans, and brown sugar. Cover and blend or process until cranberries and nuts are finely chopped; set aside.

2. In a large mixing bowl beat butter with an electric mixer on medium to high speed for 30 seconds. Add the granulated sugar, baking powder, and salt. Beat until combined, scraping sides of bowl occasionally. Beat in the eggs and orange peel until combined. Beat in as much of the flour as you can with the mixer. Using a wooden spoon, stir in any remaining flour.

3. Divide dough in half. Wrap and chill about 1 hour or until dough is easy to handle.

4. Roll half of the dough at a time between 2 sheets of waxed paper into a 10-inch square. Remove top sheet of waxed paper. Spread half of the filling over dough square to within ½ inch of edges. From one side, roll up jelly-roll style, removing waxed paper as you roll. Press edges to seal. Wrap filled roll in plastic wrap or waxed paper. Repeat with remaining dough and filling. Chill in the refrigerator for 4 hours to 24 hours.

5. Using a sharp knife, cut dough into ¼-inch-thick slices. Place slices 2 inches apart on an ungreased cookie sheet.

6. Bake in a 375° oven for 8 to 10 minutes or until edges are firm and bottoms are lightly browned. Cool on cookie sheet for 1 minute. Transfer cookies to a wire rack; cool. Makes about 60 cookies.

Nutrition facts per cookie: 85 cal., 4 g total fat (2 g sat. fat), 15 mg chol., 54 mg sodium, 11 g carbo., 0 g fiber, 1 g pro.

cornmeal-chili pepper biscotti

A sugarless cookie doesn't get any better than this! And a savory bite can be a welcome change from the holiday's sweets. Serve them as appetizers or with a steaming cup of soup.

Prep: 25 minutes   Bake: 30 to 35 minutes   Cool: 1 hour   Bake: 30 minutes

1. Lightly grease a cookie sheet; set aside.

2. In a large mixing bowl beat cheese and butter with an electric mixer on medium to high speed for 30 seconds. Add chili peppers, baking powder, salt, and pepper. Beat until combined, scraping sides of bowl occasionally. Beat in eggs. Beat in cornmeal and as much of the flour as you can with the mixer. Using a wooden spoon or your hands, stir or knead in any remaining flour.

3. Divide dough in half. Shape each half of dough into a 9-inch-long loaf. Place about 5 inches apart on the prepared cookie sheet. Flatten slightly to 3 inches wide.

4. Bake in a 350° oven for 30 to 35 minutes or until light brown. Cool on cookie sheet for 1 hour.

5. Transfer loaves to a cutting board. Cut each loaf diagonally into ½-inch-thick slices. Place slices, cut sides down, on the

cookie sheet. Bake in a 325° oven for 15 minutes. Turn slices over and bake 15 minutes more or until cookies are dry and crisp. Transfer to a wire rack; cool. Makes 28 cookies.

Nutrition facts per cookie: 76 cal., 4 g total fat (2 g sat. fat), 24 mg chol., 109 mg sodium, 8 g carbo., 0 g fiber, 3 g pro.

ingredients

1 cup shredded extra-sharp cheddar cheese (4 ounces)

¼ cup butter, softened

1 4-ounce can diced green chili peppers, drained

2½ teaspoons baking powder

¼ teaspoon salt

¼ teaspoon pepper

2 eggs

½ cup yellow cornmeal

2 cups all-purpose flour

Package a chorus of Sugar Cookie Carolers, dressed for the weather in their warm woolens, in a box or tin wrapped with holiday sheet music. As a final grace note, tie a musical instrument ornament to the bow. Or send them solo in sandwich bags of waxed paper. Fold over the top and use a paper punch to punch through all layers. Thread a ribbon through the hole to tie the bag closed.

sugar cookie carolers

The possibilities for creating this cherubic chorus of one-of-a-kind cookie faces are as limitless as your imagination.

Prep: 45 minutes   Chill: 2 to 24 hours   Bake: 6 to 8 minutes

1. In a large mixing bowl beat butter with an electric mixer on medium to high speed for 30 seconds. Add sugar, baking powder, and salt. Beat until combined, scraping sides of bowl occasionally. Beat in egg and vanilla until combined. Beat in as much of the flour as you can with the mixer. Using a wooden spoon, stir in any remaining flour.

2. Divide dough in half. Shape each half of dough into a 6-inch-long roll. Wrap in plastic wrap or waxed paper. Chill in the refrigerator for 2 to 24 hours.

3. Using a sharp knife, cut dough into ¼-inch-thick slices. (Reserve several dough slices for decorating. Tint some of dough with paste food coloring to form hats, hair, and earmuffs. Forcing dough through a garlic press will make "hair.") For each caroler's face, place a dough slice on an ungreased cookie sheet. If desired, use a straw to make an oval-shaped hole in the dough for the mouth. (It may be necessary to reform the mouth with the straw while

baked cookie is still warm.) If desired, arrange small decorative candies for the eyes and nose and add other colored dough decorations before baking.*

4. Bake in a 375° oven for 6 to 8 minutes or until edges are lightly browned. Carefully transfer cookies to a wire rack; cool. *(If desired, instead of adding candy decorations before baking, tint Powdered Sugar Icing and use a decorating bag fitted with a small plain or star tip to pipe on icing, giving each caroler eyes and a nose.) If desired, brush on red petal dust to make rosy cheeks. Makes about 40 cookies.

Powdered Sugar Icing: In a small mixing bowl stir together 1 cup sifted powdered sugar, ¼ teaspoon vanilla, and enough milk (2 to 4 teaspoons) to make icing of piping consistency. Tint with food coloring as desired.

Nutrition facts per cookie: 78 cal., 4 g total fat (2 g sat. fat), 15 mg chol., 68 mg sodium, 11 g carbo., 0 g fiber, 1 g pro.

ingredients

- ¾ cup butter, softened
- 1 cup granulated sugar
- ½ teaspoon baking powder
- ½ teaspoon salt
- 1 egg
- 1 teaspoon vanilla
- 2½ cups all-purpose flour
- Assorted colors of paste or liquid food coloring
- Small candies for decorating (optional)
- 1 recipe Powdered Sugar Icing (optional)
- Red petal dust (optional)

toasted coconut wafers

Each crisp, buttery bite celebrates the sweet taste of coconut. Make them any time of the year!

ingredients

1 cup butter, softened

1¼ cups sifted powdered sugar

½ teaspoon almond extract or vanilla

⅛ teaspoon salt

1 egg yolk

2¼ cups all-purpose flour

1 cup shredded coconut, toasted

1 beaten egg white

1½ cups shredded coconut

Prep: 25 minutes   **Chill:** 4 to 24 hours   **Bake:** 10 to 12 minutes

1. In a large mixing bowl beat butter with an electric mixer on medium to high speed for 30 seconds. Add powdered sugar, almond extract or vanilla, and salt. Beat until combined, scraping sides of bowl occasionally. Beat in egg yolk. Beat in as much of the flour as you can with the mixer. Using a wooden spoon, stir in any remaining flour and the 1 cup toasted coconut.

2. Divide dough in half. Shape each half of dough into an 8-inch-long roll. Brush rolls with egg white and roll in the 1½ cups coconut. Wrap each roll in plastic wrap or waxed paper. Chill in refrigerator for 4 to 24 hours or until firm.

3. Using a sharp knife, cut dough into ¼-inch-thick slices. Place slices 1 inch apart on an ungreased cookie sheet.

4. Bake in a 375° oven for 10 to 12 minutes or until edges are lightly browned. Cool on cookie sheet for 1 minute. Transfer cookies to a wire rack; cool. Makes about 60 cookies.

Nutrition facts per cookie: 68 cal., 4 g total fat (2 g sat. fat), 12 mg chol., 14 mg sodium, 7 g carbo., 0 g fiber, 1 g pro.

poppy seed spirals

A generous sprinkling of poppy seed gives these lemon-flavored cookies a highly distinctive, beautifully blue-hued spiral.

ingredients

- 1 cup butter, softened
- ¾ cup sugar
- ¼ teaspoon baking powder
- ⅛ teaspoon salt
- 1 egg
- 1 teaspoon vanilla
- 2⅔ cups all-purpose flour
- 3 tablespoons poppy seed
- 1 teaspoon finely shredded lemon peel

Prep: 25 minutes   Chill: 4 to 24 hours   Bake: 8 to 10 minutes

1. In a large mixing bowl beat butter with an electric mixer on medium to high speed for 30 seconds. Add sugar, baking powder, and salt. Beat until combined, scraping sides of bowl occasionally. Beat in egg and vanilla. Beat in as much of the flour as you can with the mixer. Using a wooden spoon, stir in any remaining flour.

2. Divide dough in half. Stir poppy seed and lemon peel into one dough half until combined; leave remaining half plain.

3. On a lightly floured surface, roll each half of dough into a 9×6-inch rectangle. Carefully roll poppy seed rectangle around rolling pin; unroll on top of plain rectangle. Make sure edges are aligned; press down gently with rolling pin to seal. Tightly roll up, jelly-roll style, starting from a long side. Wrap in plastic wrap. Chill for 4 to 24 hours or until very firm.

4. Using a sharp knife, cut dough into ⅛- to ¼-inch-thick slices. Place slices about 1 inch apart on an ungreased cookie sheet.

5. Bake in a 375° oven for 8 to 10 minutes or until edges are firm and lightly browned. Transfer cookies to a wire rack; cool. Makes about 48 cookies.

Nutrition facts per cookie: 74 cal., 4 g total fat (2 g sat. fat), 15 mg chol., 15 mg sodium, 8 g carbo., 0 g fiber, 1 g pro.

hickory nut and buttercream sandwiches

ingredients

- 1 cup butter, softened
- ¾ cup sugar
- 1½ teaspoons vanilla
- 1¾ cups all-purpose flour
- ¾ cup finely ground hickory nuts, pecans, or black walnuts
- ½ cup finely chopped hickory nuts, pecans, or black walnuts
- 3 ounces bittersweet chocolate, chopped (optional)
- 1 teaspoon shortening (optional)
- 1 recipe Buttercream

The rich, pecanlike hickory nut lends a touch of down-home exotica to these cream-filled, double-decker cookies.

Prep: 20 minutes   Chill: 3 to 24 hours   Bake: 12 to 15 minutes

1. In a large mixing bowl beat butter for 30 seconds. Add sugar and vanilla. Beat until combined. Beat in as much flour as you can with the mixer. Stir in any remaining flour and the ground nuts.

2. Divide dough in half. Shape each half into a 6-inch-long roll. On waxed paper, roll one dough half in ¼ cup finely chopped nuts. Repeat with remaining nuts and dough. Wrap each roll in plastic wrap or waxed paper. Chill for 3 to 24 hours. Using a sharp knife, cut dough into slightly less than ¼-inch-thick slices. Place 1 inch apart on an ungreased cookie sheet.

3. Bake in a 325° oven for 12 to 15 minutes or until bottoms of cookies are very lightly browned. Cool cookies on a wire rack.

4. If desired, in a heavy small saucepan combine chocolate and shortening. Stir over low heat until chocolate is melted. Using a small clean pastry brush, paint bottoms of half of the cookies with chocolate. Place cookies, chocolate side up, on a wire rack; let dry.

5. To assemble, spread bottoms of the plain cookies with a rounded teaspoon of Buttercream. Top with chocolate-coated cookies, chocolate side down. Chill cookies to store. Makes about 30 sandwich cookies.

Buttercream: In a small mixing bowl beat together 2 egg yolks; set aside. In a heavy small saucepan combine ⅓ cup sugar and 2 tablespoons water. Bring to boiling; remove from heat. Gradually stir about half of the sugar mixture into the egg yolks. Return entire egg yolk mixture to saucepan. Bring to a gentle boil; reduce heat. Cook and stir for 2 minutes more. Remove from heat. Stir in ½ teaspoon vanilla. Cool to room temperature. In a large mixing bowl beat ½ cup softened butter with an electric mixer on medium to high speed for 30 seconds. Add cooled sugar mixture; beat until combined. If necessary, chill until easy to spread.

Nutrition facts per cookie: 169 cal., 13 g total fat (6 g sat. fat), 39 mg chol., 63 mg sodium, 13 g carbo., 1 g fiber, 2 g pro.

A small metal screw-top canister easily holds a stack of spectacular treats—Hickory Nut and Buttercream Sandwiches. Decorate the canister with a swath of art paper and a snowflake cut from a doily and tied with ribbon or lace.

caramel-chocolate pockets

ingredients

- ¼ cup butter, softened
- ½ cup chocolate-hazelnut spread
- 1 cup sugar
- ½ teaspoon baking powder
- 1 egg
- ¼ cup milk
- 1 teaspoon vanilla
- 2½ cups all-purpose flour
- 32 vanilla or chocolate caramels (about 10 ounces)
- 2 tablespoons milk
- ¼ cup finely chopped toasted hazelnuts (filberts)

Chocolate-hazelnut spread, long popular in Europe as a bread topper for breakfast, is gaining legions of fans on these shores—and lots of new uses, too. Here, it gives great flavor to caramel-filled cookies.

Prep: 50 minutes   Chill: 4 to 24 hours   Bake: 9 to 11 minutes

1. In a large mixing bowl beat butter and chocolate-hazelnut spread with an electric mixer on medium to high speed for 30 seconds or until softened. Add sugar and baking powder. Beat until combined, scraping sides of bowl occasionally. Beat in egg, the ¼ cup milk, and vanilla until combined. Beat in as much flour as you can with the mixer. Stir in remaining flour with a wooden spoon.

2. Divide dough in half. Shape each half into a 6½-inch-long roll. Gently flatten each roll into a triangular shape. Wrap in plastic wrap or waxed paper. Chill for 4 to 24 hours.

3. For filling, in a small saucepan stir 16 of the caramels and 1 tablespoon of the milk over low heat just until melted. Cool slightly. Stir in 2 tablespoons of the nuts.

4. Reshape triangular logs, if necessary. Using a sharp knife, slice each log into slightly less than ¼-inch-thick triangles. Place half of the triangles 1 inch apart on an ungreased cookie sheet. Carefully spoon about ½ teaspoon filling atop each. Top with remaining triangles; seal edges with fork tines.

5. Bake in a 375° oven for 9 to 11 minutes or until edges are firm. Cool on cookie sheet 1 minute. Transfer cookies to a wire rack; cool.

6. For drizzle, in a small saucepan cook and stir the remaining 16 caramels and 1 tablespoon milk over low heat just until melted. Drizzle over completely cooled cookies; sprinkle with remaining nuts. Makes about 24 cookies.

Nutrition facts per cookie: 183 cal., 6 g total fat (2 g sat. fat), 14 mg chol., 79 mg sodium, 30 g carbo., 1 g fiber, 3 g pro.

84

lemon-pistachio biscotti

If you are passionate about pistachios—and it's hard not be—this very pretty cookie is the perfect vehicle for that sublime nut.

Prep: 35 minutes   **Bake:** 20 to 25 minutes
Cool: 30 minutes   **Bake:** 16 to 18 minutes

1. Line an extra-large cookie sheet or 2 cookie sheets with parchment paper or lightly grease the cookie sheet(s); set aside.

2. In a large mixing bowl beat butter with an electric mixer on medium to high speed for 30 seconds. Add sugar, baking powder, and salt; beat until combined, scraping sides of bowl occasionally. Beat in eggs and vanilla until combined. Beat in lemon peel and as much of the flour as you can with the mixer. Using a wooden spoon, stir in remaining flour and pistachio nuts.

3. On a lightly floured surface, divide dough into 3 equal portions. Shape each portion into an 8-inch-long loaf. Flatten loaves to about 2½ inches wide. Place at least 3 inches apart on prepared cookie sheet(s).

4. Bake in a 375° oven for 20 to 25 minutes or until golden brown and tops are cracked. (Loaves will spread slightly.) Cool on cookie sheet for 30 minutes.

5. Transfer loaves to a cutting board. Cut each loaf diagonally into ½-inch-thick slices. Place slices, cut sides down, on the same parchment-lined cookie sheets. Bake in a 325° oven for 8 minutes. Turn slices over and bake 8 to 10 minutes more or until dry and crisp. Transfer to a wire rack; cool. Dip ends into or drizzle with Lemon Icing. Makes about 36 cookies.

Lemon Icing: In a small mixing bowl stir together 1 cup sifted powdered sugar and 1 teaspoon finely shredded lemon peel. Stir in enough milk or lemon juice (1 to 2 tablespoons) to make icing of drizzling consistency.

Nutrition facts per cookie: 99 cal., 5 g total fat (1 g sat. fat), 16 mg chol., 71 mg sodium, 13 g carbo., 1 g fiber, 2 g pro.

ingredients

⅓ cup butter, softened
⅔ cup granulated sugar
2 teaspoons baking powder
½ teaspoon salt
2 eggs
1 teaspoon vanilla
4 teaspoons finely shredded lemon peel
2 cups all-purpose flour
1½ cups unsalted pistachio nuts (6 ounces)
1 recipe Lemon Icing

Whether they're going to trim the tree or be gobbled up, Decorated Christmas Balls make a fun gift for friends, neighbors, and co-workers. A couple of packaging ideas: Place a hot chocolate pouch, peppermint stick, and several cookies in a big holiday mug. Or, wrap two cookies back to back in cellophane and add a ribbon hanger so they may be hung from the tree (or eaten with glee).

decorated christmas balls

Kids of all ages will love to decorate these easy Christmas balls. Try colored sugars and sprinkles, gumdrops, and small candies—all of which go on before baking.

Prep: 45 minutes   Chill: 4 to 24 hours   Bake: 8 to 10 minutes

1. In a large mixing bowl beat butter and cream cheese with an electric mixer on medium to high speed for 30 seconds. Add sugar, baking powder, and salt. Beat until combined, scraping sides of bowl occasionally. Beat in egg and vanilla until combined. Beat in as much of the flour as you can with the mixer. Using a wooden spoon, stir in any remaining flour.

2. Divide dough in half. Shape each half of dough into a 7-inch-long roll. Wrap each roll in plastic wrap or waxed paper. Chill for 4 to 24 hours or until easy to handle.

3. Using a sharp knife, cut dough into ¼-inch-thick slices. Place slices about 2 inches apart on an ungreased cookie sheet. Using decorative candies, colored sugars, and/or gumdrops rolled out and cut into festive shapes, decorate the slices to resemble Christmas balls.

4. Bake in a 375° oven for 8 to 10 minutes or until edges are lightly browned. Cool on cookie sheet for 1 minute. Carefully transfer cookies to a wire rack; cool. Makes about 56 cookies.

Nutrition facts per cookie: 64 cal., 3 g total fat (2 g sat. fat), 12 mg chol., 44 mg sodium, 8 g carbo., 0 g fiber, 1 g pro.

ingredients

- ¾ cup butter, softened
- 1 3-ounce package cream cheese, softened
- ¾ cup sugar
- ½ teaspoon baking powder
- ¼ teaspoon salt
- 1 egg
- 1 teaspoon vanilla
- 2½ cups all-purpose flour
  Small multicolored decorative candies, sprinkles, gumdrops, and assorted colored sugars

visions of sugar plums

Bedeck frosted cookies with candy ornaments crafted from gumdrops. Here are three ideas. Use your imagination to conjure up some more.

Bells: Cut a large gumdrop lengthwise into 4 slices. Add a red cinnamon candy along the long flat side of each slice of the gumdrop to form a bell.

Cutouts: Use your fingers or a rolling pin to flatten a gumdrop to about ⅛-inch thickness. Cut out small shapes using a knife or hors d'oeuvres cutters.

Holly leaves: Arrange slices of small green gumdrops around red cinnamon candies to create holly and berries.

pealing bells

These buttery Christmas bells may be soundless, but they're sure to delight your senses of sight and taste.

ingredients

  1 cup butter, softened

  1 cup granulated sugar

  2 tablespoons milk

  1 teaspoon vanilla

2½ cups all-purpose flour

 ½ cup colored sugar or
      nonpareils (optional)

30 maraschino cherries,
      halved and well
      drained, or small
      candies

Prep: 30 minutes   Chill: 4 to 24 hours   Bake: 12 to 14 minutes

1. In a large mixing bowl beat butter with an electric mixer on medium to high speed for 30 seconds. Add granulated sugar. Beat until combined, scraping sides of bowl occasionally. Beat in milk and vanilla until combined. Beat in as much of the flour as you can. Using a wooden spoon, stir in any remaining flour.

2. Divide dough in half. Shape each half of dough into an 8-inch-long roll. If desired, roll in colored sugar or nonpareils to coat. Wrap each roll in plastic wrap or waxed paper. Chill for 4 to 24 hours.

3. Using a sharp knife, cut dough into ¼-inch-thick slices. Place slices on an ungreased cookie sheet. Fold in sides of each slice, overlapping where they meet; pinch in sides to create a bell shape.

4. Bake in a 350° oven for 12 to 14 minutes or until edges are firm. Immediately press a cherry half or small candy at the bottom of each slice for a bell clapper. Transfer cookies to a wire rack; cool. Makes about 60 cookies.

Nutrition facts per cookie: 62 cal., 3 g total fat (2 g sat. fat), 8 mg chol., 31 mg sodium, 8 g carbo., 0 g fiber, 1 g pro.

spiced mice

After they've been nestled snug in the cookie jar for safekeeping, the only stirring these sweet creatures will do will be caused by hungry, treat-seeking hands.

Prep: 30 minutes   **Chill:** 5 to 24 hours   **Bake:** 8 to 10 minutes

1. In a large mixing bowl beat butter and shortening with an electric mixer on medium to high speed for 30 seconds. Add granulated sugar, brown sugar, pumpkin pie or apple pie spice, and baking soda. Beat until combined, scraping sides of bowl occasionally. Beat in egg and vanilla until combined. Beat in as much of the flour as you can with the mixer. Using a wooden spoon, stir in any remaining flour.

2. Shape dough into a 9-inch-long roll about 2 inches in diameter. Wrap in plastic wrap or waxed paper. Chill in the refrigerator for 5 to 24 hours or until firm enough to slice.

3. Using a sharp knife, cut roll into ¼-inch-thick slices. Cut each slice in half. Cut each candy bar into 12 rectangles or cut mint candies in half crosswise. For one mouse, place a half slice on an ungreased cookie sheet. Top the half slice with 1 chocolate bar rectangle. Place a chow mein noodle on one side, close to the flat edge, so it resembles a tail. Top with a second half slice. Gently press edges of

slices together to seal. Gently press an almond slice into the cookie for an ear. Press in candy-coated chocolate pieces for an eye and nose. Repeat with remaining cookies and ingredients, placing cookies about 2 inches apart on the cookie sheet.

4. Bake in a 375° oven for 8 to 10 minutes or until edges are golden. Cool on the cookie sheet for 1 minute. Carefully transfer cookies to a wire rack; cool. Makes 36 cookies.

Nutrition facts per cookie: 126 cal., 7 g total fat (3 g sat. fat), 14 mg chol., 43 mg sodium, 14 g carbo., 0 g fiber, 1 g pro.

ingredients

½ cup butter, softened

½ cup shortening

½ cup granulated sugar

½ cup packed brown sugar

1¼ teaspoons pumpkin pie spice or apple pie spice

¼ teaspoon baking soda

1 egg

½ teaspoon vanilla

2¼ cups all-purpose flour

3 1.4 to 1.55-ounce bars white chocolate with crisped rice cereal, white chocolate with chocolate cookie pieces, or milk chocolate, or 18 layered chocolate-mint candies

36 almond slices

36 chow mein noodles

72 miniature candy-coated milk chocolate pieces

italian fig spirals

ingredients

⅓ cup butter, softened

1 cup sugar

½ teaspoon baking powder

1 egg

3 tablespoons milk

½ teaspoon vanilla

2½ cups all-purpose flour

1 cup finely snipped dried figs

⅓ cup orange marmalade

¼ cup orange juice

Fig cookies at Christmas are as Italian as opera. Sculpt these cookies into the shape of figs before they're baked by pinching and narrowing a portion of each slice.

Prep: 35 minutes   Chill: 5 to 24 hours   Bake: 9 to 11 minutes

1. In a large mixing bowl beat butter with an electric mixer on medium to high speed for 30 seconds. Add sugar and baking powder. Beat until combined, scraping sides of bowl occasionally. Beat in egg, milk, and vanilla until combined. Beat in as much of the flour as you can with the mixer. Using a wooden spoon, stir in any remaining flour. Cover; chill 1 hour or until dough is easy to handle.

2. Meanwhile, for filling, in a small saucepan combine figs, marmalade, and orange juice. Cook and stir just until boiling. Remove from heat and cool.

3. Divide dough in half. On waxed paper use a floured rolling pin to roll half of the dough at a time into a 10×8-inch rectangle. Spread half of the filling over dough rectangle to within ½ inch of edges. From one short side, roll up jelly-roll style, removing waxed paper as you roll. Pinch edges to seal. Wrap filled roll in plastic wrap or waxed paper. Repeat with remaining dough and filling. Chill in the refrigerator for 4 to 24 hours.

4. Line a cookie sheet with foil. Grease the foil; set aside.

5. Using a sharp knife, cut filled dough rolls into ¼-inch-thick slices. Place slices 2 inches apart on prepared cookie sheet. Form each slice into a fig shape, if desired.

6. Bake in a 375° oven for 9 to 11 minutes or until edges are firm and bottoms are lightly browned. Transfer cookies to a wire rack; cool. Makes 60 cookies.

Nutrition facts per cookie: 54 cal., 1 g total fat (1 g sat. fat), 6 mg chol., 15 mg sodium, 11 g carbo., 1 g fiber, 1 g pro.

Italian Fig Spirals look lovelier still when offered in something colorful. Here, an elegant glass pedestal dish with cranberry-colored accents works nicely. If you'd like, add color to the outside of a plain glass dish by painting on details with glass paint or gluing on gems with epoxy.

walnut-chocolate squares

Chocolate and toasted nuts pair up in a rich cookie that's great with a cup of coffee. With either vanilla or chocolate icing, embellish the toothsome tile-shaped treats with pretty patterns or geometric mosaics.

Prep: 25 minutes   Chill: 4 to 24 hours   Bake: 8 to 10 minutes

ingredients

1 cup butter, softened

1 cup granulated sugar

⅓ cup unsweetened cocoa
    powder

1 teaspoon vanilla

⅛ teaspoon salt

1 cup toasted walnuts,
    pecans, or hazelnuts
    (filberts), finely ground

2¼ cups all-purpose flour

1 recipe Vanilla or
    Chocolate Icing

1. In a medium mixing bowl beat butter with an electric mixer on medium to high speed for 30 seconds. Add sugar, cocoa powder, vanilla, and salt. Beat until combined, scraping sides of bowl occasionally. Beat in the ground nuts and as much of the flour as you can with the mixer. Using a wooden spoon, stir in remaining flour.

2. Shape dough on a large piece of waxed paper or plastic wrap into a 10×2-inch square log. Wrap in plastic wrap or waxed paper. Chill in the refrigerator for 4 to 24 hours.

3. Line a cookie sheet with parchment paper or lightly grease a cookie sheet.

4. Using a sharp knife, cut dough into slightly less than ¼-inch-thick slices. Place slices 1 inch apart on prepared cookie sheet.

5. Bake in a 350° oven for 8 to 10 minutes or until cookies look dry. Transfer cookies to a wire rack; cool. Decorate cookies as desired with Vanilla and/or Chocolate Icing. Makes about 48 cookies.

Vanilla Icing: In a small mixing bowl stir together 1 cup sifted powdered sugar, ¼ teaspoon vanilla, and enough milk (about 1 to 2 tablespoons) to make icing of drizzling consistency.

Chocolate Icing: In a small mixing bowl stir together 1 cup sifted powdered sugar, 3 tablespoons unsweetened cocoa powder, ¼ teaspoon vanilla, and enough milk (about 1 to 2 tablespoons) to make icing of drizzling consistency.

Nutrition facts per cookie: 97 cal., 6 g total fat (3 g sat. fat), 10 mg chol., 12 mg sodium, 11 g carbo., 0 g fiber, 1 g pro.

lemon candy cookies

These are for the real lemon-lover in your crowd. They can be made with orange or cherry candies, too.

Prep: 25 minutes   Chill: 5 hours   Bake: 9 to 11 minutes

1. In a large mixing bowl beat butter with an electric mixer on medium to high speed for 30 seconds. Add sugar and baking powder. Beat until combined, scraping sides of bowl occasionally. Beat in egg and lemon peel until combined. Beat in as much of the flour as you can with the mixer. Using a wooden spoon, stir in any remaining flour.

2. Divide dough in half. Stir yellow food coloring and lemon candies into one half of dough; mix until combined. Leave remaining portion of the dough plain. Divide each half of dough in half again, making a total of 4 portions. Cover; chill dough portions about 1 hour or until dough is easy to handle.

3. Between 2 sheets of waxed paper, roll one portion of the yellow dough into a 9×8-inch rectangle. Repeat with a portion of the plain dough. Remove top sheets of waxed paper from both dough rectangles. Carefully invert yellow dough over plain dough. Remove top sheet of waxed paper.

4. Starting from one of the 8-inch sides, tightly roll up jelly-roll style, removing waxed paper as you roll. Pinch edges to seal. Wrap in plastic wrap or waxed paper. Repeat with remaining portions of dough. Chill about 4 hours or until firm.

5. Unwrap chilled dough and reshape slightly, if necessary. Using a sharp knife, cut dough into ¼-inch-thick slices. Place slices 2 inches apart on an ungreased cookie sheet.

6. Bake in a 375° oven for 9 to 11 minutes or until edges are firm and lightly browned. Cool on the cookie sheet for 1 minute. Transfer cookies to a wire rack; cool. Makes about 60 cookies.

Cherry Candy Cookies: Prepare cookies as directed above, except substitute ¼ teaspoon almond extract for the lemon peel, red food coloring for the yellow, and cherry candies for the lemon candies.

Nutrition facts per cookie: 60 cal., 3 g total fat (2 g sat. fat), 12 mg chol., 35 mg sodium, 8 g carbo., 0 g fiber, 1 g pro.

ingredients

  1 cup butter, softened

  1 cup sugar

  ½ teaspoon baking powder

  1 egg

1½ teaspoons finely shredded lemon peel or orange peel

2¼ cups all-purpose flour

  9 to 12 drops yellow food coloring (plus 2 drops red if making orange cookies)

  ⅓ cup finely crushed hard lemon candies or orange candies

A handful of Cherry-Almond Slices wrapped in plastic wrap and tucked into a pretty teapot or teacup, along with a few envelopes of special tea, makes a terrific gift for the tea-lover on your list. Or, fill a set of wine glasses with these cookies and place them in a basket along with a bottle of sparkling juice.

cherry-almond slices

Consider these preserve-filled cookies with a biscuitlike texture for part of a lovely light breakfast that includes a pot of hot tea.

Prep: 25 minutes   Bake: 25 to 30 minutes   Cool: 1 hour

1. Line a cookie sheet with foil; set aside.

2. In a large mixing bowl beat butter with an electric mixer on medium to high speed for 30 seconds. Add brown sugar, baking powder, and salt. Beat until combined, scraping sides of bowl occasionally. Beat in eggs and kirsch or orange juice until combined. Beat in as much of the flour as you can with the mixer. Using a wooden spoon, stir in any remaining flour and ¼ cup of the finely chopped almonds.

3. Divide dough in half. Shape each half of dough into a 9-inch-long log. Place on prepared cookie sheet. Flatten to 1 inch thick. Make an indentation that's 1 inch wide and ½ inch deep down the middle of each log from end to end. Combine egg yolk and milk. Brush on top and sides of

logs. Spoon cherry preserves in the indentations. Sprinkle with remaining finely chopped nuts.

4. Bake in a 375° oven for 25 to 30 minutes or until a wooden toothpick inserted near the center comes out clean. Cool logs on the cookie sheet on a wire rack about 1 hour. Transfer logs to a cutting board. With a serrated knife, cut each log crosswise into ½-inch-thick slices.

5. Freeze slices for storage. If desired, in a small saucepan melt chocolate and shortening over low heat. Drizzle over the slices before serving. Makes about 36 cookies.

Nutrition facts per cookie: 81 cal., 4 g total fat (2 g sat. fat), 25 mg chol., 40 mg sodium, 11 g carbo., 0 g fiber, 1 g pro.

ingredients

½ cup butter, softened
⅓ cup packed brown sugar
½ teaspoon baking powder
Dash salt
2 eggs
1 tablespoon kirsch or orange juice
2¼ cups all-purpose flour
⅓ cup finely chopped toasted almonds
1 egg yolk
1 tablespoon milk
½ cup cherry preserves
1 ounce bittersweet chocolate, chopped (optional)
¼ teaspoon shortening (optional)

lemon-poppy seed melts

If you're planning to freeze these melt-in-your-mouth cookies, leave the powdered sugar off. You can shake them in powdered sugar once you've taken them out of the freezer and they've thawed.

Prep: 20 minutes   **Chill:** 4 to 24 hours   **Bake:** 7 to 9 minutes

ingredients

½ cup butter, softened

½ cup granulated sugar

1 tablespoon poppy seed

⅛ teaspoon baking soda

1 egg yolk

1 tablespoon milk

2 teaspoons finely shredded lemon peel

½ teaspoon vanilla

1½ cups all-purpose flour

1 cup sifted powdered sugar

Yellow edible glitter (optional)

1. In a medium mixing bowl beat butter with an electric mixer on medium to high speed for 30 seconds Add the granulated sugar, poppy seed, and baking soda. Beat until combined, scraping sides of bowl occasionally. Beat in the egg yolk, milk, lemon peel, and vanilla until combined. Beat in as much of the flour as you can with the mixer. Using a wooden spoon, stir in any remaining flour.

2. Divide dough in half. Shape each half of dough into a 9-inch-long roll. Wrap each roll in plastic wrap or waxed paper. Chill in the refrigerator for 4 to 24 hours.

3. Using a sharp knife, cut dough into ½-inch-thick slices. Place slices 1 inch apart on an ungreased cookie sheet.

4. Bake in a 375° oven for 7 to 9 minutes or until edges are firm and bottoms of cookies are lightly browned.

5. Place powdered sugar in a plastic bag. If desired, add edible glitter to powdered sugar. While cookies are still warm, transfer several at a time to the bag of powdered sugar. Gently shake until coated. Transfer cookies to a wire rack. When completely cool, gently shake cookies again in the powdered sugar. Makes about 36 cookies.

Nutrition facts per cookie: 64 cal., 3 g total fat (2 g sat. fat), 13 mg chol., 31 mg sodium, 9 g carbo., 0 g fiber, 1 g pro.

rounder slices

Do your sliced cookies look more like flat tires than full moons? Sometimes perfectly round rolls of cookie dough flatten and become misshapen while chilling. Keep your cookie dough in a perfect cylinder while it's chilling by sliding the roll of dough into a tall drinking glass or a baguette pan. While you're slicing, rotate the roll frequently to avoid creating a flat side.

maple-pecan biscotti

Two indigenous ingredients—maple syrup and pecans—give an American accent to a classic Italian cookie.

Prep: 20 minutes   Chill: 1 hour   Bake: 25 to 30 minutes
Cool: 1 hour   Bake: 16 to 18 minutes

1. In a large mixing bowl beat butter with an electric mixer on medium to high speed for 30 seconds. Add sugar and baking powder. Beat until combined, scraping sides of bowl occasionally. Beat in eggs, maple syrup, and vanilla until combined. Beat in as much of the flour as you can with the mixer. Using a wooden spoon, stir in any remaining flour and the 1 cup toasted chopped pecans.

2. Divide dough in half. If necessary, cover and chill for 1 hour or until easy to handle.

3. Lightly grease a cookie sheet; set aside.

4. Shape each half of dough into a 9-inch-long loaf. Place 4 inches apart on prepared cookie sheet. Flatten loaves slightly. Sprinkle with the ⅓ cup finely chopped pecans; press into tops of loaves. Flatten loaves to about 3 inches wide.

5. Bake in a 375° oven for 25 to 30 minutes or until a wooden toothpick inserted near the center comes out clean. Cool loaves on cookie sheet on a wire rack for 1 hour. Transfer to a cutting board. With a serrated knife, cut each loaf diagonally into ½-inch-thick slices. Place slices, cut sides down, on an ungreased cookie sheet.

6. Bake in a 325° oven for 8 minutes. Turn slices over; bake for 8 to 10 minutes more or until dry and crisp. Transfer to a wire rack; cool. Drizzle with Maple Drizzle. Makes about 24 cookies.

Maple Drizzle: In a small mixing bowl stir together 1¼ cups sifted powdered sugar and 1 tablespoon maple syrup. Stir in additional maple syrup (4 to 5 tablespoons) to make icing of drizzling consistency.

Nutrition facts per cookie: 172 cal., 7 g total fat (2 g sat. fat), 25 mg chol., 62 mg sodium, 26 g carbo., 1 g fiber, 2 g pro.

ingredients

- ⅓ cup butter, softened
- ½ cup granulated sugar
- 2 teaspoons baking powder
- 2 eggs
- ¼ cup maple syrup
- ½ teaspoon vanilla
- 2¾ cups all-purpose flour
- 1 cup toasted chopped pecans
- ⅓ cup finely chopped pecans
- 1 recipe Maple Drizzle

snickerdoodle pinwheels

ingredients

⅓ cup sugar

1 tablespoon ground cinnamon

½ cup butter, softened

1 3-ounce package cream cheese, softened

1 cup sugar

½ teaspoon baking powder

1 egg

1 teaspoon vanilla

2⅔ cups all-purpose flour

1 tablespoon butter, melted

A whirl of cinnamon is at the center of this crisp cookie inspired by the homey flavor of one of America's favorite native treats.

Prep: 25 minutes   Chill: 4 hours   Bake: 8 to 10 minutes

1. For cinnamon-sugar mixture, in a small bowl combine the ⅓ cup sugar and the cinnamon; set aside.

2. In a large mixing bowl beat the ½ cup butter and the cream cheese with an electric mixer on medium to high speed for 30 seconds. Add the 1 cup sugar and baking powder. Beat until combined, scraping sides of bowl occasionally. Beat in egg and vanilla until combined. Beat in as much of the flour as you can with the mixer. Using a wooden spoon, stir in remaining flour.

3. Divide dough in half. Roll half of dough between 2 sheets of waxed paper into a 12×8-inch rectangle. Remove top sheet of waxed paper. Brush dough with half of the melted butter. Sprinkle with 2 tablespoons of the cinnamon-sugar mixture.

4. Starting from one of the short sides, roll up jelly-roll style, removing waxed paper as you roll. Seal edges. Repeat with remaining dough, butter, and 2 tablespoons of the cinnamon-sugar mixture. Roll each log in remaining cinnamon-sugar mixture. Wrap each log in plastic wrap or waxed paper. Chill in the refrigerator about 4 hours or until firm.

5. Using a sharp knife, cut dough into ¼-inch-thick slices. Place slices 1 inch apart on an ungreased cookie sheet.

6. Bake in a 375° oven for 8 to 10 minutes or until edges are firm. Cool on cookie sheet for 1 minute. Transfer to a wire rack; cool. Makes about 60 cookies.

Nutrition facts per cookie: 57 cal., 2 g total fat (1 g sat. fat), 10 mg chol., 26 mg sodium, 8 g carbo., 0 g fiber, 1 g pro.

Transform an ordinary paper cup into a cheery vessel for bestowing treats simply by rubber stamping it with a seasonal motif. Add holes around the top of the cup with a small paper punch. (You can use these same stamping and punching techniques on a paper lunch bag.)

SWEET SPOONFULS

Light someone's day with a gift of these pistachio-studded cookies packed in a beaded basket tied with a sheer organdy ribbon. Or, to create a lovely hostess gift, place the cookies in a beribboned wire mesh basket with a pretty pillar candle in the center.

chocolate-cherry drops

Get the colors of Christmas—red tart cherries and green-hued pistachios—in every delightful bite of these cookies. If you prefer other dried fruits to the cherries, try snipped dried apricots or golden raisins.

Prep: 30 minutes   Bake: 10 to 12 minutes

1. Lightly grease a cookie sheet; set aside.

2. In a large mixing bowl beat butter with an electric mixer on medium to high speed for 30 seconds. Add granulated sugar, brown sugar, and baking soda. Beat until combined, scraping sides of bowl occasionally. Beat in the melted unsweetened chocolate, eggs, and vanilla until combined. Beat in as much of the flour as you can with the mixer. Using a wooden spoon, stir in any remaining flour, the cherries, and the 1 cup pistachio nuts.

3. Drop dough by rounded teaspoon about 2 inches apart onto the prepared cookie sheet.

4. Bake in a 350° oven for 10 to 12 minutes or until edges are firm. Cool on cookie sheet for 1 minute. Transfer cookies to a wire rack; cool.*

5. In a small saucepan melt white baking bars and shortening over low heat, stirring frequently. Drizzle over cookies. Immediately sprinkle with finely chopped pistachios. Makes 40 cookies.

*Note: If they're not going to be eaten within 2 days, the cookies should be stored in the freezer at this point. To serve, thaw, drizzle with melted baking bars mixture, and sprinkle with nuts.

Nutrition facts per cookie: 155 cal., 9 g total fat (4 g sat. fat), 24 mg chol., 85 mg sodium, 18 g carbo., 1 g fiber, 2 g pro.

ingredients

- 1 cup butter, softened
- ¾ cup granulated sugar
- ¾ cup packed brown sugar
- 1 teaspoon baking soda
- 3 ounces unsweetened chocolate, melted and cooled slightly
- 2 eggs
- 1 teaspoon vanilla
- 2 cups all-purpose flour
- 1½ cups snipped dried tart cherries
- 1 cup pistachio nuts
- 3 ounces white baking bars
- 2 teaspoons shortening
- ¼ cup very finely chopped pistachio nuts

yield to the right

Does your actual cookie yield come up short when checked against the one stated in the recipe? If so, you're probably using too much dough per cookie. To drop dough by rounded teaspoons, use spoons from your flatware (not measuring spoons or flatware soup or serving spoons) to scoop the dough. The dough should fill a spoon with a nicely rounded top. If you prefer a larger cookie, scoop a little more dough and allow 1 or 2 minutes more for baking. You'll wind up with fewer cookies.

sesame cookies

Make these tender cookies infused with nutty-tasting toasted sesame oil and toasted sesame seed ahead. They freeze beautifully.

Prep: 20 minutes   **Bake:** 7 to 9 minutes

ingredients

1½ cups butter, softened

1 cup sugar

1 teaspoon baking powder

½ teaspoon ground ginger

1 egg

2 tablespoons milk

½ teaspoon toasted
      sesame oil

½ teaspoon vanilla

3 cups all-purpose flour

⅔ cup toasted sesame seed

1. In a large mixing bowl beat butter with an electric mixer on medium to high speed for 30 seconds. Add sugar, baking powder, and ginger. Beat until combined, scraping sides of bowl occasionally. Beat in egg, milk, sesame oil, and vanilla. Beat in as much of the flour as you can with the mixer. Using a wooden spoon, stir in any remaining flour and ¼ cup of the sesame seed.

2. Drop dough by rounded teaspoon 2 inches apart onto an ungreased cookie sheet. Sprinkle with remaining sesame seed.

3. Bake in a 375° oven for 7 to 9 minutes or until edges are golden. Transfer cookies to a wire rack; cool. Makes about 96 cookies.

Nutrition facts per cookie: 53 cal., 3 g total fat (2 g sat. fat), 10 mg chol., 34 mg sodium, 5 g carbo., 0 g fiber, 1 g pro.

toasting sesame seed

Southern cooks have been stirring sesame seed (sometimes called benne seed) into buttery rich cookie doughs for generations. In fact, some Southerners insist that eating these tiny, pearly white seeds will bring good luck. Although you may notice no change in fortune, you won't question the wonderful flavor they impart to cookies. Toasting further enhances the slightly sweet, nutty taste.

   To toast sesame seed, spread them in a shallow, ungreased pan. Heat in a 350° oven for 10 to 15 minutes, stirring once or twice.

orange-pumpkin cookies

This moist little cookie packs great pumpkin flavor that's beautifully complemented by an orange-butter frosting.

Prep: 30 minutes **Bake:** 9 to 11 minutes

1. In a large mixing bowl beat butter and shortening with an electric mixer on medium to high speed for 30 seconds. Add the granulated sugar, brown sugar, baking powder, and baking soda. Beat until combined, scraping sides of bowl occasionally. Beat in orange peel, egg, and pumpkin. Beat in as much of the flour as you can with the mixer. Using a wooden spoon, stir in any remaining flour.

2. Drop dough by rounded teaspoon 2 inches apart onto an ungreased cookie sheet.

3. Bake in a 375° oven for 9 to 11 minutes or until tops are firm. Transfer cookies to a wire rack; cool. When cool, frost with Orange-Butter Frosting. If desired, garnish each frosted cookie with sugared, finely shredded orange peel. Makes 36 cookies.

Orange-Butter Frosting: In a medium mixing bowl beat ¼ cup butter until fluffy. Gradually add 2 cups sifted powdered sugar, beating well. Slowly beat in ¾ teaspoon finely shredded orange peel and 2 tablespoons orange juice. Beat in additional orange juice, if needed, to make frosting of spreading consistency.

Nutrition facts per cookie: 128 cal., 7 g total fat (3 g sat. fat), 16 mg chol., 55 mg sodium, 16 g carbo., 0 g fiber, 1 g pro.

ingredients

- ½ cup butter, softened
- ½ cup shortening
- ½ cup granulated sugar
- ½ cup packed brown sugar
- ½ teaspoon baking powder
- ¼ teaspoon baking soda
- 1 teaspoon finely shredded orange peel
- 1 egg
- 1 cup canned pumpkin
- 2 cups all-purpose flour
- 1 recipe Orange-Butter Frosting

  Sugared, finely shredded orange peel (optional)

sachertorte cookies

ingredients

2 cups all-purpose flour

⅓ cup unsweetened cocoa powder

1 teaspoon baking powder

¼ teaspoon baking soda

¼ teaspoon salt

¼ cup butter, softened

¼ cup cooking oil

1 cup packed brown sugar

⅓ cup granulated sugar

2 ounces unsweetened chocolate, melted and cooled slightly

1 teaspoon vanilla

3 eggs

1 8-ounce carton dairy sour cream

½ cup apricot preserves

1 recipe Chocolate Frosting

1 cup milk chocolate pieces

1 teaspoon shortening

Viennese pastry chefs often pipe the word Sacher *atop the classic chocolate-and-apricot torte to identify it as the real thing. These mini versions may only have room for an S, but they're just as special.*

Prep: 50 minutes   Bake: 8 to 10 minutes

1. Lightly grease a cookie sheet; set aside.

2. In a medium bowl combine flour, cocoa powder, baking powder, baking soda, and salt; set aside.

3. In a large mixing bowl beat butter with an electric mixer on medium to high speed for 30 seconds. Add oil, brown sugar, granulated sugar, unsweetened chocolate, and vanilla. Beat until combined, scraping sides of bowl occasionally. Add eggs one at a time, beating well after each addition. Beat in sour cream until combined. Beat in as much of the flour mixture as you can with the mixer on low speed. Using wooden spoon, stir in remaining flour mixture.

4. Drop dough by rounded teaspoon 2 inches apart onto the prepared cookie sheet.

5. Bake in a 375° oven for 8 to 10 minutes or until tops spring back when pressed lightly. Transfer cookies to a wire rack; cool.*

6. In a small saucepan melt apricot preserves over low heat. Force preserves through a strainer with the back of a wooden spoon, discarding any large pieces. Brush tops of cooled cookies with strained preserves. Frost cookies with Chocolate Frosting. In a heavy small saucepan melt milk chocolate pieces and shortening over low heat. Pipe or drizzle a letter S on each cookie. Place on wire rack; let stand until set. Store cookies in refrigerator for up to 3 days. Makes about 60 cookies.

Chocolate Frosting: In a heavy small saucepan melt 8 ounces semisweet chocolate and 2 tablespoons butter over low heat, stirring frequently. Remove pan from heat and stir in 2 tablespoons light-colored corn syrup and 2 tablespoons milk. Whisk until smooth.

Note: Cookies can be frozen at this point for later use. To serve, thaw, brush with preserves, frost, and decorate.

Nutrition facts per cookie: 109 cal., 6 g total fat (3 g sat. fat), 15 mg chol., 42 mg sodium, 14 g carbo., 0 g fiber, 2 g pro.

Inspired as Sachertorte Cookies are by their namesake torte, a small antique cake stand makes a grand presentation (and present) for these cookies. If you prefer, personalize the underside of a new glass cake stand with glass paint. For a contemporary look, try winding the stem of a stand with beaded copper wire. For a Victorian touch, place a small paper doily under each cookie; then wind delicate lace or ribbon between them.

tropical jumbles

ingredients

- ½ cup butter, softened
- ½ cup shortening
- 1¼ cups packed brown sugar
- ½ teaspoon baking soda
- 2 eggs
- 1 teaspoon vanilla
- 2½ cups all-purpose flour
- 1 3½-ounce jar macadamia nuts, chopped (about 1 cup)
- 1 cup shredded or flaked coconut
- ½ cup chopped candied pineapple, or raisins, or snipped dried apricots
- ½ cup chopped dried papaya or mango
- ½ cup dried banana chips, broken (optional)
- 1 recipe Citrus Glaze

There may not be snow for Christmas, but these treats, packed with macadamia nuts, coconut, and fruit prove that on the cookie front, tropics-dwellers aren't missing a thing!

Prep: 25 minutes   **Bake:** 8 to 10 minutes

1. In a large mixing bowl beat butter and shortening with an electric mixer on medium to high speed for 30 seconds. Add brown sugar and baking soda. Beat until combined, scraping sides of bowl occasionally. Beat in eggs and vanilla until combined. Beat in as much of the flour as you can with the mixer. Using a wooden spoon, stir in any remaining flour. Stir in macadamia nuts, coconut, pineapple, papaya, and, if using, banana pieces.

2. Drop dough by rounded teaspoon 2 inches apart onto an ungreased cookie sheet.

3. Bake in a 375° oven for 8 to 10 minutes or until edges are lightly browned. Transfer cookies to a wire rack; cool. When cool, drizzle with Citrus Glaze. Makes about 60 cookies.

Citrus Glaze: In a medium mixing bowl stir together 2 cups sifted powdered sugar and enough orange, lemon, or lime juice (2 to 3 tablespoons) to make glaze of drizzling consistency. Tint bright yellow, orange, or blue-green with food coloring for a tropical look. Or, if desired, divide the glaze into portions and tint each portion with a different color of food coloring.

Nutrition facts per cookie: 100 cal., 5 g total fat (2 g sat. fat), 11 mg chol., 30 mg sodium, 13 g carbo., 0 g fiber, 1 g pro.

fruit and spice rounds

Chopping the dried fruits in a food processor with a little of the flour to keep the bits from sticking makes light work of these old-world-style spice cookies.

Prep: 40 minutes   Bake: 12 to 15 minutes

1. In large mixing bowl beat butter with an electric mixer on medium to high speed about 30 seconds. Add sugar, baking powder, cinnamon, nutmeg, and cloves. Beat until combined, scraping sides of bowl occasionally. Beat in eggs until combined. Beat in as much of the flour as you can with the mixer. Using a wooden spoon, stir in any remaining flour. Stir in raisins, figs, dates, and nuts.

2. Drop dough by rounded teaspoon 2 inches apart onto an ungreased cookie sheet.

3. Bake in 350° oven for 12 to 15 minutes or until edges are lightly browned. Cool on cookie sheet for 1 minute. Transfer cookies to a wire rack; cool. When cookies are cool, drizzle with Browned Butter Icing. Makes 54 cookies.

Browned Butter Icing: In a heavy small saucepan melt ⅓ cup butter over low heat. Continue heating until butter turns a delicate golden brown. Remove from heat; pour into a medium bowl. Add 3 cups sifted powdered sugar, 4 teaspoons milk, and ½ teaspoon vanilla. Beat with an electric mixer on low speed until combined. Beat on medium to high speed, adding a little additional milk, if needed, to make icing of drizzling consistency.

Nutrition facts per cookie: 136 cal., 6 g total fat (3 g sat. fat), 24 mg chol., 61 mg sodium, 22 g carbo., 1 g fiber, 1 g pro.

ingredients

- 1   cup butter, softened
- 1½ cups granulated sugar
- 1½ teaspoons baking powder
- 1   teaspoon ground cinnamon
- ½   teaspoon ground nutmeg
- ½   teaspoon ground cloves
- 3   eggs
- 2   cups all-purpose flour
- 1   cup raisins, snipped
- 1   cup dried figs, snipped
- 1   cup snipped pitted dates
- ½   cup chopped walnuts
- 1   recipe Browned Butter Icing

drop cookie basics

Keep these points in mind for perfect drop cookies:

- Drop dough into rounded mounds of the same size so they'll bake evenly.
- Leave enough space between cookies to keep them from spreading into one another.
- Drop cookies are done when the dough looks set and the edges and bottoms of the baked cookies are lightly browned.

Coffee and cookies make a perfect pair for gift-giving. Nestle a few Coffee Crisps in an oversize java cup filled with coffee beans. Or wrap cookies individually in plastic wrap and stack them in a clean coffee bean bag. For "just a little something," put one or two cookies in a basket-type paper coffee filter. Use a paper punch to punch holes about every inch around the top of the filter. Weave a ribbon through the holes and cinch the top closed.

coffee crisps

Coffee in the dough and a coffee-and-cream icing give these cookies great cappuccino flavor. Serve them with (what else?) a great cup of steaming hot java.

Prep: 25 minutes   Bake: 9 to 11 minutes

1. Line cookie sheet with parchment paper; set the cookie sheet aside.

2. In a small bowl stir together water and coffee crystals or espresso coffee powder until dissolved; set aside.

3. In a large mixing bowl beat butter with an electric mixer on medium to high speed for 30 seconds. Add sugar and salt. Beat until combined, scraping sides of bowl occasionally. Add eggs and coffee mixture; beat until combined. Beat in as much of the flour as you can with the mixer. Using a wooden spoon, stir in any remaining flour.

4. Drop dough by slightly rounded teaspoon 2 inches apart onto the prepared cookie sheet; spread dough into 2-inch circles.

5. Bake in a 350° oven for 9 to 11 minutes or until browned around the edges. Cool on cookie sheet set on a wire rack for 2 minutes. Transfer cookies to wire rack; cool.

6. When cookies are cool, fill a pastry bag fitted with a very small round tip with Coffee Icing. Pipe icing onto cookies in a zigzag pattern. Or, thin icing with additional whipping cream to make icing of drizzling consistency; use fork tines to drizzle icing over cookies. If desired, sprinkle with crushed coffee crystals. Makes about 20 cookies.

Coffee Icing: Stir together ⅛ teaspoon instant coffee crystals or dash of espresso coffee powder and 1 tablespoon whipping cream until coffee is dissolved. In a small mixing bowl stir together 1 cup sifted powdered sugar, the coffee-cream mixture, and enough additional whipping cream (1 to 2 tablespoons) to make icing of piping consistency.

Nutrition facts per cookie: 143 cal., 6 g total fat (3 g sat. fat), 36 mg chol., 61 mg sodium, 22 g carbo., 0 g fiber, 2 g pro.

ingredients

- 4 teaspoons water
- 2 teaspoons instant coffee crystals or 1 teaspoon instant espresso coffee powder
- ½ cup butter, softened
- 1 cup granulated sugar
- ¼ teaspoon salt
- 2 eggs
- 1½ cups all-purpose flour
- 1 recipe Coffee Icing
  Instant coffee crystals, coarsely crushed (optional)

peanut brittle cookies

Here's the best of both worlds: cookies and candy. These peanut-studded sweets feature crunchy, buttery peanut brittle encased in a soft, chewy oatmeal cookie.

Prep: 20 minutes   Bake: 12 to 13 minutes

ingredients

½ cup butter, softened

¼ cup shortening

1 cup packed dark
      brown sugar

½ teaspoon baking powder

¼ teaspoon baking soda

1 egg

1 teaspoon vanilla

1¼ cups all-purpose flour

1¼ cups quick-cooking
      rolled oats

4 ounces bittersweet or
      semisweet chocolate,
      chopped

1 cup crushed peanut
      brittle

1. Line 2 cookie sheets with foil and grease the foil; set aside.

2. In a large mixing bowl beat butter and shortening with an electric mixer on medium to high speed for 30 seconds. Add brown sugar, baking powder, and baking soda. Beat until combined, scraping sides of bowl occasionally. Beat in egg and vanilla until combined. Beat in as much of the flour as you can with the mixer. Using a wooden spoon, stir in any remaining flour. Stir in the rolled oats, chopped chocolate, and ½ cup of the crushed peanut brittle.

3. Drop dough by rounded teaspoon 2 inches apart onto the prepared cookie sheets. Flatten each mound slightly.

4. Bake in a 350° oven for 8 minutes. Remove cookie sheet from oven. Sprinkle with remaining ½ cup crushed peanut brittle, carefully pressing in slightly. Bake for 4 to 5 minutes longer or until edges are lightly browned. Cool on cookie sheet for 2 minutes. Transfer cookies to a wire rack; cool. Makes about 24 cookies.

Nutrition facts per cookie: 175 cal., 9 g total fat (4 g sat. fat), 19 mg chol., 67 mg sodium, 23 g carbo., 1 g fiber, 3 g pro.

truffle cookies

Simpler to make than true truffles—but every bit as rich and fudgy—these triple-chocolate treats will satisfy the palate of the most discriminating cocoa-fiend.

Prep: 30 minutes   **Bake:** 7 to 9 minutes

1. In a heavy medium saucepan melt the 8 ounces chopped bittersweet chocolate and butter over low heat, stirring frequently. Add eggs, brown sugar, granulated sugar, flour, the 2 tablespoons cocoa powder, the vanilla, and baking powder. Stir until combined, scraping sides of pan occasionally. Stir in the 6 ounces chopped bittersweet chocolate.

2. Drop dough by slightly rounded teaspoon 1 inch apart onto an ungreased cookie sheet.

3. Bake in a 325° oven for 7 to 9 minutes or until edges are firm and surfaces are dull. Do not overbake. Transfer cookies to a wire rack; cool. If desired, sift cocoa powder or powdered sugar over the tops before serving. Makes 48 cookies.

Nutrition facts per cookie: 63 cal., 4 g total fat (2 g sat. fat), 11 mg chol., 15 mg sodium, 8 g carbo., 1 g fiber, 1 g pro.

ingredients

8 ounces bittersweet chocolate, chopped

3 tablespoons butter

2 eggs

½ cup packed brown sugar

¼ cup granulated sugar

¼ cup all-purpose flour

2 tablespoons unsweetened cocoa powder

1 teaspoon vanilla

½ teaspoon baking powder

6 ounces bittersweet chocolate, chopped

Unsweetened cocoa powder or powdered sugar (optional)

almond sweets

ingredients

- 3 cups all-purpose flour
- 1 tablespoon baking powder
- ½ teaspoon salt
- 3 eggs
- ½ cup granulated sugar
- ½ cup cooking oil
- 1 teaspoon vanilla
- 1 recipe Almond Icing
- Small multicolored decorative candies (optional)

Despite the name, this Italian-style cookie is not overly sweet, making it a great addition to any holiday cookie tray.

Prep: 35 minutes   Bake: 12 to 15 minutes

1. Lightly grease a cookie sheet; set aside.

2. In a medium bowl stir together flour, baking powder, and salt. In a large mixing bowl beat eggs, sugar, oil, and vanilla with an electric mixer until combined. Beat in as much of the flour mixture as you can with the mixer. Using a wooden spoon, stir in any remaining flour mixture.

3. Drop dough by rounded teaspoon 2 inches apart onto the prepared cookie sheet.

4. Bake in a 350° oven for 12 to 15 minutes or until golden. Transfer cookies to a wire rack; cool. When cookies are cool, spread with Almond Icing. Sprinkle lightly with multicolored candies, if desired. Makes about 60 cookies.

Almond Icing: In a medium mixing bowl stir together 1 cup sifted powdered sugar, ½ teaspoon almond extract, and 1 to 2 tablespoons milk to make icing of spreading consistency. Tint with food coloring, if desired.

Nutrition facts per cookie: 54 cal., 2 g total fat (0 g sat. fat), 11 mg chol., 39 mg sodium, 8 g carbo., 0 g fiber, 1 g pro.

A Christmas ornament box keeps these sweets safely stored until you can share them with a friend. Line each compartment with tissue paper or shredded crinkle paper before adding the cookies. String beaded garland through the box as an additional gift.

FESTIVE BARS AND BROWNIES

peanut butter and chocolate chip bars

ingredients

¾ cup peanut butter

¼ cup cooking oil

1 cup packed brown sugar

2 eggs

½ teaspoon baking powder

¼ teaspoon baking soda

1 cup all-purpose flour

¾ cup milk

¾ cup rolled oats

½ cup miniature semisweet chocolate pieces

⅓ cup chopped peanuts

Purchased frosting

Assorted small candies

As pretty as any ornament on the tree (and edible to boot!), these yummy treats will razzle-dazzle kids of all ages.

Prep: 20 minutes   Bake: 25 to 30 minutes

1. Grease a 13×9×2-inch baking pan; set aside.

2. In a large mixing bowl beat peanut butter and oil with an electric mixer on low to medium speed for 30 seconds. Add brown sugar, eggs, baking powder, and baking soda. Beat until combined, scraping sides of bowl occasionally. Beat in flour; then beat in the milk. Using a wooden spoon, stir in rolled oats, chocolate pieces, and peanuts. Spread batter in prepared pan.

3. Bake in a 350° oven for 25 to 30 minutes or until a wooden toothpick inserted near center comes out clean. Cool completely in pan on a wire rack.

4. Cut into triangles, circles, and squares that are about 2½ inches across (reserve end pieces for nibbling). Decorate shapes with purchased frosting and candies so they look like drums, presents, and trees. Makes about 16 bars.

Nutrition facts per bar: 270 cal., 15 g total fat (3 g sat. fat), 27 mg chol., 125 mg sodium, 31 g carbo., 2 g fiber, 7 g pro.

Treats as ornamental as these deserve outstanding packaging. Share a sample in a box that has been wrapped in a striking gift wrap, lid and all. Or, have the kids decorate a box with stickers, buttons, and snippets of lace and ribbon for interest. Be sure to line the box with colored tissue paper, waxed paper, or heavy cellophane before filling it with goodies.

chocolate-cherry-toffee bars

Topped with artfully arranged red and green candied cherries, these rich bars are a festive addition to any holiday cookie assortment.

ingredients

¾ cup butter, softened

¾ cup packed brown sugar

1 egg yolk

1½ cups all-purpose flour

1 cup finely chopped candied cherries

¼ teaspoon salt

1 14-ounce can (1¼ cups) sweetened condensed milk

2 tablespoons butter

1 cup semisweet chocolate pieces

20 candied red cherries, cut in half

    Candied green cherries (optional)

Prep: 35 minutes   Bake: 32 minutes

1. Line a 13×9×2-inch baking pan with foil; set aside.

2. In a large mixing bowl beat the ¾ cup butter and brown sugar with an electric mixer on medium to high speed until combined. Add egg yolk; beat well. Using a wooden spoon, stir in flour, the 1 cup candied cherries, and salt; mix well. With floured hands, press dough into the prepared pan.

3. Bake in a 350° oven about 20 minutes or until lightly golden. Transfer pan to a wire rack.

4. Meanwhile, for topping, in a heavy medium saucepan heat sweetened condensed milk and the 2 tablespoons butter over medium heat until bubbly, stirring constantly. Stir in chocolate pieces until smooth. Spread over hot baked layer.

5. Bake for 12 minutes more. Place 40 red cherry halves on top, spacing them evenly. Add slivers of candied green cherry "leaves," if desired. Cool in pan on wire rack. Cover and chill. Lift foil out of pan; cut into bars. Makes 40 bars.

Nutrition facts per bar: 137 cal., 6 g total fat (3 g sat. fat), 19 mg chol., 68 mg sodium, 20 g carbo., 0 g fiber, 2 g pro.

foiled!

If your bar cookies play tricks on you by sticking to the baking pan, try lining the pan with foil. It may save you a tad on cleanup, too.

Tear off a foil piece bigger than the pan. Press it in the pan, extending it over the pan's edges slightly. If a recipe calls for a greased pan, grease the foil. Spread the dough evenly in the pan. Bake and cool the bars in the pan; then pull the foil edges down to the counter and lift the bars out. Cut into bars, squares, triangles, or diamonds.

golden fig diamonds

Dried fruits have long been the centerpiece of wintertime baking and a boon to creative holiday cooks. These Italian-style fig cookies celebrate tradition with a citrus twist.

Prep: 30 minutes   **Bake:** 50 minutes

1. Lightly grease an 8×8×2-inch baking pan; set aside.

2. For filling, in a medium saucepan combine figs, ½ teaspoon orange peel, orange juice, brown sugar, and cinnamon. Bring to boiling; reduce heat. Simmer, uncovered, stirring frequently, over medium-low heat about 5 minutes or until figs are soft and mixture begins to thicken (mixture will thicken more while cooling). Remove from heat; stir in ½ teaspoon vanilla. Cool completely; set aside.

3. For crust, in a large mixing bowl beat butter with an electric mixer on medium to high speed for 30 seconds. Add the ½ cup granulated sugar, ½ teaspoon vanilla, and salt, and beat until combined. Beat in as much of the flour as you can with the mixer. Stir in any remaining flour (mixture will be crumbly). Set aside ¾ cup of the mixture for topping. Using your fingers, press remaining mixture evenly into bottom of the prepared pan.

4. Bake in a 350° oven about 20 minutes or until edges are golden brown. Spread cooled fig mixture on top of hot crust. Sprinkle reserved crust mixture over filling. In a small bowl combine the 1 tablespoon sugar and ½ teaspoon orange peel; sprinkle on top.

5. Bake about 30 minutes more or until crust is golden brown. Cool completely in pan on a wire rack.

6. To cut the bars in a diamond shape, cut parallel lines 1¼ inches apart down the length of the pan. Then cut diagonal lines 1¼ inches apart across the pan. Top bars with orange peel twists, if desired. Makes about 18 bars.

Nutrition facts per bar: 147 cal., 5 g total fat (3 g sat. fat), 14 mg chol., 33 mg sodium, 25 g carbo., 2 g fiber, 1 g pro.

ingredients

- 8   ounces dried Calimyrna (golden) figs, chopped (1½ cups)
- ½   teaspoon finely shredded orange peel
- ¾   cup orange juice
- ¼   cup packed brown sugar
     Dash ground cinnamon
- ½   teaspoon vanilla
- ½   cup butter, softened
- ½   cup granulated sugar
- ½   teaspoon vanilla
- ⅛   teaspoon salt
- 1⅓ cups all-purpose flour
- 1   tablespoon granulated sugar
- ½   teaspoon finely shredded orange peel
     Orange peel twists (optional)

Serve up a few of these buttery Butterscotch Shortbread Bars in a pewter kitchen scoop that's perfect for gift-giving. Tie the handle with a handmade gift tag of layered papers (the largest one could contain the recipe) or with a beautiful bow. Or, instead of a scoop, use a new or antique flour sifter or measuring cups.

butterscotch shortbread bars

The only thing better than buttery shortbread is buttery shortbread crowned with a topping of butterscotch and nuts. Half confection, half cookie, these sweet treats are 100 percent delicious.

Prep: 25 minutes   Bake: 37 to 40 minutes

1. Line a 9×9×2-inch baking pan with foil; extend foil over pan edges. Butter foil; set aside.

2. For crust, in a medium mixing bowl combine flour, the 3 tablespoons brown sugar, and the baking powder. Using a pastry blender, cut in the ½ cup butter until mixture resembles coarse crumbs. Press crust mixture into the prepared pan. Bake in a 350° oven for 25 minutes or until golden brown.

3. Meanwhile, for butterscotch sauce, in a heavy medium saucepan melt the ¼ cup butter. Stir in granulated sugar, the ⅓ cup brown sugar, corn syrup, water,

and salt; stir in the chopped cashews. Bring to boiling over medium-high heat, stirring constantly. Boil, uncovered, for 5 minutes, stirring often. Remove saucepan from heat. Stir in whipping cream and vanilla.

4. Spread butterscotch mixture evenly over the baked crust. Bake for 12 to 15 minutes more or until most of the surface is bubbly. Cool in pan on a wire rack. Lift foil out of pan; cut into bars. Makes 24 bars.

Nutrition facts per bar: 152 cal., 10 g total fat (5 g sat. fat), 19 mg chol., 108 mg sodium, 16 g carbo., 0 g fiber, 2 g pro.

ingredients

1¼ cups all-purpose flour

3 tablespoons brown sugar

¼ teaspoon baking powder

½ cup butter

¼ cup butter

⅓ cup granulated sugar

⅓ cup packed brown sugar

⅓ cup light-colored corn syrup

1 tablespoon water

¼ teaspoon salt

½ cup coarsely chopped walnuts

½ cup coarsely chopped cashews

¼ cup whipping cream

1 teaspoon vanilla

pumpkin cheesecake bars

ingredients

- 2 cups finely crushed gingersnaps (about 30 cookies)
- ¼ cup butter, melted
- ⅓ cup canned pumpkin
- 1 tablespoon all-purpose flour
- 1 teaspoon pumpkin pie spice
- 3 8-ounce packages cream cheese, softened
- 1 cup sugar
- 1½ teaspoons vanilla
- 3 eggs

*A **spicy gingersnap crust** is the perfect foil for the rich, creamy pumpkin cheesecake filling. The most crisp gingersnaps you can find will produce the best crust.*

Prep: 20 minutes   Bake: 35 to 40 minutes

1. Lightly grease a 13×9×2-inch baking pan; set aside.

2. For crust, in a small bowl combine gingersnaps and melted butter. Press evenly into bottom of the prepared pan. Bake in a 325° oven about 10 minutes or until crust is firm; cool.

3. Meanwhile, for pumpkin batter, in a medium bowl stir together pumpkin, flour, and pumpkin pie spice until combined; set aside.

4. For cream cheese batter, in a large mixing bowl beat cream cheese until smooth. Add sugar and vanilla, beating until combined. Add eggs, one at a time, beating at low speed with an electric mixer after each addition just until combined. Stir ⅓ of the cream cheese batter (about 1½ cups) into the pumpkin batter until smooth. Pour remaining cream cheese batter over crust. Place large spoonfuls of pumpkin batter randomly over cream cheese batter. Using the tip of a table knife or a thin metal spatula, gently swirl the two batters together. Bake for 25 to 30 minutes more or until center is just set.

5. Cool completely in pan on a wire rack. Cover and chill for 4 to 24 hours before cutting into squares or bars. Store any remaining bars in the refrigerator. Makes 24 bars.

Nutrition facts per bar: 199 cal., 13 g total fat (8 g sat. fat), 63 mg chol., 163 mg sodium, 17 g carbo., 0 g fiber, 3 g pro.

candy bar brownies

As candymakers discovered long ago, getting chocolate in your peanut butter or peanut butter on your chocolate can be a very good thing. The two complementary tastes make these tri-level bars a winner.

Prep: 25 minutes   **Bake:** 25 minutes

1. For crust, in a medium mixing bowl combine graham crackers, the ¼ cup sugar, and the ¼ cup finely chopped peanuts. Stir in the ½ cup melted butter. Press mixture evenly into the bottom of an ungreased 11×7×1½-inch baking pan. Bake in a 350° oven for 5 minutes; cool.

2. For filling, in a heavy large saucepan melt the remaining ½ cup butter and chocolate over low heat, stirring occasionally. Remove from heat; stir in the 1 cup sugar, eggs, and vanilla. Stir just until combined. Stir in flour and peanut butter-flavored pieces. Spread evenly over crust.

3. Bake for 20 minutes more. Cool completely in pan on a wire rack. Spread with Peanut Butter Frosting. Cut into 1-inch squares. Place a peanut half on each square. Place in small candy cups, if desired. (If desired, cut into 24 larger bars.) Makes 70 bite-size brownies.

Peanut Butter Frosting: In a medium mixing bowl beat ¼ cup butter and 2 tablespoons peanut butter with an electric mixer on low speed for 30 seconds. Gradually add 1 cup sifted powdered sugar, beating well. Beat in 1 tablespoon milk and ½ teaspoon vanilla. Gradually beat in 1 cup additional sifted powdered sugar and enough milk to make frosting of spreading consistency.

Nutrition facts per bite-sized bar: 83 cal., 5 g total fat (3 g sat. fat), 15 mg chol., 53 mg sodium, 10 g carbo., 0 g fiber, 1 g pro.

ingredients

1¼ cups finely crushed graham crackers (about 18 graham crackers)

¼ cup granulated sugar

¼ cup finely chopped dry-roasted peanuts

½ cup butter, melted

½ cup butter

2 ounces unsweetened chocolate, cut up

1 cup granulated sugar

2 eggs

1 teaspoon vanilla

⅔ cup all-purpose flour

½ cup peanut butter-flavored pieces

1 recipe Peanut Butter Frosting

¼ cup peanut halves

visions-of-sugar-plums pizza

ingredients

⅔ cup butter, softened

¾ cup sugar

1 teaspoon ground ginger

½ teaspoon baking soda

½ teaspoon ground cinnamon

1 egg

2 tablespoons molasses

1¾ cups all-purpose flour

1¾ cups halved small and/or cut-up large gumdrops

½ cup white baking pieces

1½ teaspoons butter-flavor or regular shortening

These bejeweled treats will surely set little ones to sweet-dreaming. A hint: Smaller gumdrops usually are spicy and larger ones usually are not. If you prefer, you can use jelly beans or other small candies.

Prep: 20 minutes   Bake: 20 minutes

1. Lightly grease a 12- or 13-inch pizza pan or a 13×9×2-inch baking pan; set aside.

2. In a large mixing bowl beat butter with an electric mixer on medium to high speed for 30 seconds. Add sugar, ginger, baking soda, and cinnamon. Beat until combined, scraping sides of bowl occasionally. Beat in egg and molasses until combined. Beat in as much of the flour as you can with the mixer. Using a wooden spoon, stir in any remaining flour.

3. Spread the dough evenly into the prepared pan.

4. Bake in a 350° oven for 12 minutes. Sprinkle partially baked cookie with gumdrops. Return to oven. Bake about 8 minutes more or until edges are browned (do not overbake). Cool completely in pan on a wire rack.

5. In a heavy small saucepan melt white baking pieces and shortening over low heat. Drizzle over cookie. Let stand about 20 to 30 minutes or until set. To serve, cut into wedges or bars. Makes 16 wedges.

Nutrition facts per wedge: 232 cal., 10 g total fat (6 g sat. fat), 36 mg chol., 131 mg sodium, 33 g carbo., 0 g fiber, 2 g pro.

Give this sweet pizza tied
with a string licorice bow
to your favorite kid. For friends
or neighbors, put the cookie
pizza on top of a pizza stone
and wrap it in a fanciful
kitchen towel tied with
a bow. Attach a pizza cutter
to round out the gift.

eggnog squares

ingredients

2 cups sugar

⅔ cup butter

2 eggs

1 teaspoon vanilla

2 cups all-purpose flour

1 teaspoon baking powder

¾ teaspoon ground nutmeg

½ cup flaked coconut

Nutmeg-spiced eggnog—that creamy and cool Yuletide treat—is the essence of these coconut-studded bars that are just perfect with a cup of hot coffee or tea.

Prep: 20 minutes   **Bake:** 25 to 30 minutes

1. Grease a 13×9×2-inch baking pan; set aside.

2. In a medium saucepan cook and stir sugar and butter over medium heat until butter melts; cook and stir 2 minutes more. Cool 10 minutes. Using a wooden spoon, stir in eggs one at a time; stir in vanilla. Stir in flour, baking powder, and nutmeg until combined. Stir in coconut. Spread mixture evenly into the prepared pan.

3. Bake in a 350° oven for 25 to 30 minutes or until edges just begin to pull away from pan. Cool in pan on a wire rack. Makes 36 bars.

Nutrition facts per bar: 106 cal., 4 g total fat (3 g sat. fat), 21 mg chol., 49 mg sodium, 17 g carbo., 0 g fiber, 1 g pro.

a pan in hand

A pan in hand may be worth two in the bush, but not if it's the wrong size. Fortunately, you can swap pans in a pinch.

- If you don't have a 15×10×1-inch pan, use two 9×9×2-inch baking pans.
- If you don't have a 13×9×2-inch pan, use two 8×8×2-inch baking pans.

In both substitutions, use the same oven temperature, but check the bars for doneness 5 minutes before the minimum baking time given in the recipe is reached.

pear mince streusel bars

Christmas wouldn't be Christmas without mince, but who has time for pie when there's so much cookie-baking to do? These easy bars featuring a fresh pear mince let you have your cake and eat it, too.

Prep: 30 minutes   Bake: 32 to 37 minutes

1. Prepare Fresh Pear Mince Filling. Set aside to cool slightly.

2. Meanwhile, for crust, in a large mixing bowl beat butter with an electric mixer on medium to high speed for 30 seconds. Add the granulated sugar, brown sugar, and baking soda. Beat until combined, scraping sides of bowl occasionally. Beat in as much of the flour as you can with the mixer. Using a wooden spoon, stir in any remaining flour until mixture is crumbly. Reserve 1 cup of the mixture for topping.

3. Press remaining crust mixture into the bottom of an ungreased 13×9×2-inch baking pan. Bake in a 375° oven for 12 minutes or until golden.

4. Carefully spread Fresh Pear Mince Filling evenly over crust. Combine the 1 cup reserved crust mixture and walnuts; sprinkle over filling. Bake for 20 to 25 minutes more or until golden. Cool in pan on a wire rack. Cut into bars. Store up to 3 days in the refrigerator; freeze for longer storage. Makes 32 bars.

Fresh Pear Mince Filling: In a medium saucepan combine 3 medium pears (1 pound), peeled, cored, and coarsely chopped (about 3 cups chopped); ⅓ cup dried currants or snipped raisins; ¼ cup packed brown sugar; 2 tablespoons brandy or orange juice; ½ teaspoon ground cinnamon; and ½ teaspoon ground nutmeg. Bring to boiling, stirring constantly; reduce heat. Simmer, uncovered, for 5 minutes or until pear pieces are tender, stirring occasionally. Remove from heat.

Nutrition facts per bar: 131 cal., 7 g total fat (4 g sat. fat), 15 mg chol., 79 mg sodium, 16 g carbo., 1 g fiber, 1 g pro.

ingredients

  1   recipe Fresh Pear
       Mince Filling
  1   cup butter, softened
  ⅓   cup granulated sugar
  ⅓   cup packed brown sugar
  ½   teaspoon baking soda
 2½   cups all-purpose flour
  ½   cup chopped walnuts

129

Taking a break for tea and sweets is welcome respite from garden chores. An empty clay bulb-forcing pot filled with several individually wrapped Apricot Linzer Bars makes a great gift for your favorite green thumb. Or tuck the wrapped bars inside a brand-new pair of gardening gloves and fill the pot with paperwhite bulbs.

apricot linzer bars

The traditional raspberry-and-almond flavor combination of the lattice-crusted Viennese dessert linzertorte sweetly steps aside for apricots and hazelnuts in these sophisticated but simple-to-make bars.

Prep: 25 minutes   Bake: 35 to 40 minutes

1. Grease and lightly flour an 11×7×1½-inch baking pan; set aside.

2. Place hazelnuts in a blender container or food processor bowl. Cover and blend or process until nuts are ground. Stir flour into ground hazelnuts; set aside.

3. For batter, in a large mixing bowl beat butter with an electric mixer on medium to high speed for 30 seconds. Add granulated sugar, cocoa powder, cinnamon, cloves, and salt. Beat until combined, scraping sides of bowl occasionally. Beat in egg and egg yolk until combined. Beat in as much of the flour-nut mixture as you can with the mixer. Using a wooden spoon, stir in any remaining flour-nut mixture.

4. Evenly spread about 2 cups of the batter into the prepared pan. Spoon apricot preserves over batter to within ½ inch of edges. Drop remaining batter by spoonfuls over the preserves.

5. Bake in 350° oven for 35 to 40 minutes or until lightly browned and a wooden toothpick inserted into batter comes out clean. Cool completely in pan on a wire rack. Sift powdered sugar over top before cutting into bars. Store in the refrigerator or freezer. Makes 15 to 24 bars.

Nutrition facts per bar (15): 258 cal., 15 g total fat (6 g sat. fat), 53 mg chol., 43 mg sodium, 30 g carbo., 1 g fiber, 3 g pro.

ingredients

- 1 cup hazelnuts (filberts)
- 1¼ cups all-purpose flour
- ¾ cup butter, softened
- 1 cup granulated sugar
- 4 teaspoons unsweetened cocoa powder
- ¾ teaspoon ground cinnamon
- ¼ to ½ teaspoon ground cloves
- ⅛ teaspoon salt
- 1 egg
- 1 egg yolk
- ½ cup apricot preserves
  Powdered sugar

OLD-WORLD
FAVORITES

zaletti

ingredients

- ¾ cup dried currants
- 2 tablespoons dark rum
- ⅔ cup butter, softened
- ⅔ cup sugar
- 1 teaspoon baking powder
- ¼ teaspoon salt
- 1 egg
- 2 teaspoons finely shredded orange peel
- ½ cup yellow cornmeal
- 1½ cups all-purpose flour
- Sugar

In the Veneto (Venice) region of Italy, these crunchy cookies are made with polenta—coarsely ground cornmeal—which could account for their name. In Venetian dialect, zaletti *means "little yellow things."*

Prep: 1 hour   Chill: 3 hours   Bake: 6 to 8 minutes

1. In a small bowl combine currants and rum; cover and let stand 30 minutes.

2. In a large mixing bowl beat butter with an electric mixer on medium to high speed for 30 seconds. Add the ⅔ cup sugar, baking powder, and salt. Beat until combined, scraping sides of bowl occasionally. Beat in egg and orange peel until combined. Beat in cornmeal and as much of the flour as you can with the mixer. Using a wooden spoon, stir in currant mixture and any remaining flour.

3. Divide dough in half. Wrap each half in waxed paper or plastic wrap. Chill in the refrigerator for 3 hours or until dough is easy to handle.

4. On a lightly floured surface, roll half of the dough at a time into a 12×8-inch rectangle. Using a knife, cut dough rectangle diagonally into diamond shapes 3 inches long and 1¼ inches wide. Place diamonds 1 inch apart on an ungreased cookie sheet. Sprinkle lightly with additional sugar.

5. Bake in a 375° oven for 6 to 8 minutes or until edges are lightly browned. Transfer cookies to a wire rack; cool. Makes about 54 cookies.

Nutrition facts per cookie: 56 cal., 2 g total fat (1 g sat. fat), 10 mg chol., 41 mg sodium, 8 g carbo., 0 g fiber, 1 g pro.

For a lover of country style, tie up small bundles of Zaletti with gingham ribbon and give them in an antique salad mold. Or, place a piece of cotton print fabric between two clear glass plates and arrange the cookies side by side on the top plate to reflect a quilt pattern.

christmas fig cookies

All of the ingredients that give these moist cookies their Sicilian flair—figs, citrus, and almonds—are native to that tiny island and find their way into many of its Christmas sweets.

Prep: 45 minutes   Chill: 3 hours   Bake: 10 to 12 minutes

ingredients

½   cup butter, softened
¼   cup granulated sugar
¼   cup packed brown sugar
¼   teaspoon baking soda
1   egg
1   teaspoon vanilla
1¾ cups all-purpose flour
1   recipe Fig Filling
1   recipe Lemon Glaze or
       powdered sugar

1. In a medium mixing bowl beat butter with an electric mixer on medium to high speed for 30 seconds. Add the ¼ cup granulated sugar, the brown sugar, and baking soda. Beat until combined, scraping sides of bowl occasionally. Beat in egg and vanilla until combined. Beat in as much of the flour as you can with the mixer. Using a wooden spoon, stir in remaining flour. Divide dough in half. Cover and chill about 3 hours or until dough is easy to handle. Meanwhile, prepare Fig Filling.

2. On a floured pastry cloth, roll one dough portion at a time into a 10×8-inch rectangle. Cut each rectangle into two 10×4-inch strips. Divide Fig Filling among the four strips; spread it lengthwise down the middle of each. Using cloth as a guide, lift up one long side of dough and fold it over the filling. Lift up opposite side and fold it over to enclose filling; seal edges. Place filled strips on an ungreased cookie sheet, seam sides down.

3. Bake in a 375° oven for 10 to 12 minutes or until lightly browned.

Immediately slice each strip diagonally into 1-inch pieces. Transfer pieces to a wire rack; cool. Drizzle with Lemon Glaze or sift powdered sugar over tops. Makes about 36 cookies.

Fig Filling: In a small saucepan combine 1 cup dried figs (stems removed and figs chopped); ⅔ cup raisins, finely chopped; ½ cup orange juice; ⅓ cup diced candied fruits and peels, finely chopped; 2 tablespoons granulated sugar; 1 teaspoon finely shredded lemon peel; and ¼ teaspoon ground cinnamon. Bring just to boiling; reduce heat. Cover and simmer for 5 to 8 minutes or until fruit is softened and mixture is thick; stir occasionally. Stir in ⅓ cup blanched almonds, finely chopped. Cool mixture to room temperature.

Lemon Glaze: In small mixing bowl stir together ¾ cup sifted powdered sugar and enough lemon juice (2 to 3 teaspoons) to make glaze of drizzling consistency.

Nutrition facts per cookie: 102 cal., 3 g total fat (2 g sat. fat), 13 mg chol., 38 mg sodium, 17 g carbo., 1 g fiber, 1 g pro.

mantecados

An egg glaze brushed on right before baking gives these Spanish lemon-and-almond-flavored biscuits a beautiful shine.

Prep: 30 minutes **Chill:** 1 hour **Bake:** 8 to 10 minutes

1. In a large mixing bowl beat butter with an electric mixer on medium to high speed for 30 seconds. Add sugar and lemon peel and beat until combined. Beat in as much of the flour as you can with the mixer. Using a wooden spoon, stir in any remaining flour. Stir in ground almonds. (Mixture may seem dry at first. If necessary, knead gently with your hands until mixture clings together.) Form into a ball.

2. Divide dough in thirds. Cover and chill about 1 hour or until dough is firm.

3. On a lightly floured surface, roll one portion of dough at a time to slightly less than ¼-inch thickness. Using cookie cutters, cut dough into rounds, crescents, squares, or stars. Place cookies on an ungreased cookie sheet. Beat together egg and water; brush mixture over tops of the cookies.

4. Bake in a 350° oven for 8 to 10 minutes or until edges are lightly browned. Cool on cookie sheet for 1 minute. Transfer cookies to a wire rack; cool. Makes 50 to 60 cookies.

Nutrition facts per cookie: 73 cal., 4 g total fat (2 g sat. fat), 14 mg chol., 39 mg sodium, 8 g carbo., 0 g fiber, 1 g pro.

ingredients

1 cup butter, softened

1 cup sugar

1 tablespoon finely shredded lemon peel

2 cups all-purpose flour

½ cup blanched almonds, very finely ground

1 egg

1 teaspoon water

You might just save someone's day with a gift of buttery Berlinerkranzen set atop a raftlike gift tray crafted of candy sticks. Simply cut a piece of medium-weight cardboard or foam-core board to the desired width and 1 inch shorter than the candy sticks. Attach the candy sticks to the cardboard with Royal Icing (page 16). When dry, fill in between the sticks with additional Royal Icing.

berlinerkranzen

In Germany the word kranz *means "wreath" or "garland." In Denmark, these Norwegian "butter knot" cookies are called* vanillekranser.

Prep: 30 minutes   Chill: 1 hour   Bake: 18 to 20 minutes

1. In a large mixing bowl beat butter with an electric mixer on medium to high speed for 30 seconds. Add powdered sugar; beat until combined. Beat in hard-cooked and raw egg yolks and vanilla. Beat in as much of the flour as you can with the mixer. Using a wooden spoon, stir in any remaining flour.

2. Cover and chill dough about 1 hour or until firm enough to handle. (Chilling it longer may make it too firm to roll.)

3. On a lightly floured surface, using about 1 tablespoon dough for each cookie, roll dough into 6-inch-long ropes. On an ungreased cookie sheet shape each rope into a ring, crossing it over itself about 1 inch from ends. Brush with egg white and sprinkle with pearl or coarse sugar.

4. Bake in a 325° oven for 18 to 20 minutes or until edges are lightly browned. Cool on cookie sheet for 1 minute. Transfer cookies to a wire rack; cool. Makes about 36 cookies.

Nutrition facts per cookie: 83 cal., 5 g total fat (3 g sat. fat), 25 mg chol., 54 mg sodium, 8 g carbo., 0 g fiber, 1 g pro.

ingredients

- 1 cup butter, softened
- ½ cup sifted powdered sugar
- 1 hard-cooked egg yolk, sieved
- 1 raw egg yolk
- 1 teaspoon vanilla
- 2¼ cups all-purpose flour
- 1 slightly beaten egg white
- 2 to 3 tablespoons pearl or coarse sugar

spiced chocolate macaroons

The flavor of these cinnamon-and-spiced chocolate meringue cookies from Basel, Switzerland, improves as they age—that is, if they have a chance to do so.

Prep: 20 minutes   Bake: 10 to 12 minutes

ingredients

8   ounces blanched almonds (1⅓ cups)
1   cup sugar
1½ teaspoons ground cinnamon
½   teaspoon ground cloves
4   ounces unsweetened or semisweet chocolate, chopped
2   egg whites
1   tablespoon kirsch or water
¼   cup sugar

1. Line a cookie sheet with parchment paper; set aside.

2. In a food processor bowl fitted with metal blade combine almonds, the 1 cup sugar, cinnamon, and cloves. Cover and process just until nuts are finely ground; add chocolate. Cover and process until chocolate is finely grated, but not melted. Add egg whites and kirsch or water. Process until dough just clings together.

3. Place the ¼ cup sugar in a small bowl. Form dough into 1-inch balls (dough will be sticky). Roll balls in the ¼ cup sugar to coat.

4. Place balls 2 inches apart on prepared cookie sheet. Flatten balls to about ¼-inch thickness using the bottom of a glass.

5. Bake in a 325° oven for 10 to 12 minutes or until tops are set but centers remain moist; do not overbake. Transfer cookies to a wire rack; cool. Makes about 48 cookies.

Nutrition facts per cookie: 61 cal., 4 g total fat (1 g sat. fat), 0 mg chol., 3 mg sodium, 7 g carbo., 1 g fiber, 1 g pro.

krumkake

Eat them plain, or for a special treat, pipe the finished paper-thin cookies full of sweetened whipped cream and serve immediately.

Prep: 25 minutes   Cook: 30 seconds per cookie

1. In a saucepan melt butter; cool slightly.

2. In a medium mixing bowl beat eggs with an electric mixer on medium speed about 1 minute. Add sugar; beat about 3 minutes or until sugar is almost dissolved. Stir butter into egg mixture. Add flour, vanilla or almond extract, and nutmeg; stir just until smooth.

3. Heat a krumkake iron on the range top over medium-low heat. For a 6-inch iron, spoon about 1 tablespoon of the batter onto the hot, ungreased iron. Close gently but firmly. Cook over medium-low heat about 30 seconds. Open iron carefully. Loosen cookie with a narrow spatula; invert onto a wire rack. Immediately roll the cookie around a metal cone or cylinder. Let cookie cool around the cone or cylinder until it holds the shape.

4. Reheat the iron and repeat with remaining batter. Cool rolled cookies on a wire rack. Makes 24 cookies.

Nutrition facts per cookie: 68 cal., 4 g total fat (3 g sat. fat), 37 mg chol., 47 mg sodium, 6 g carbo., 0 g fiber, 1 g pro.

ingredients

½ cup butter

3 eggs

½ cup sugar

½ cup all-purpose flour

1 teaspoon vanilla
    or ½ teaspoon
    almond extract

Dash ground nutmeg

austrian cookie tarts

ingredients

1 recipe Browned Butter
  Spice Dough
1 recipe Plain Butter Dough
½ cup raspberry or apricot
  preserves
Sifted powdered sugar

Inspired by ischlerkrapferl—*an Austrian sandwich cookie made with two different nut doughs—these two-tone cookies made with a spice dough and a plain dough get more delicious with a few days' aging.*

Prep: 25 minutes   Chill: 1 hour   Bake: 7 to 8 minutes

1. On a lightly floured surface, roll each portion of dough to ⅛-inch thickness. Using 2½- to 3-inch cookie cutters with scalloped edges, cut dough into shapes. (Make matching cutout shapes from each dough.) Using ½-inch aspic cutters, cut 3 shapes from center of each Plain Butter Dough cutout (do not make cutouts in Browned Butter Spice Dough). Place 1 inch apart on an ungreased cookie sheet.

2. Bake in a 375° oven for 7 to 8 minutes or until edges are very lightly browned. Transfer cookies to a wire rack; cool.

3. To assemble, spread about 1 teaspoon preserves on bottom of each Browned Butter Spice cookie. Top each with a Plain Butter cookie, bottom side down. Just before serving, generously sift powdered sugar atop. Makes about 20 sandwich cookies.

Browned Butter Spice Dough: In a small saucepan heat ½ cup butter over medium heat until butter turns color of light brown sugar. Remove from heat. Pour into a medium bowl; chill until butter resolidifies. Beat browned butter on medium to high speed for 30 seconds. Add ½ cup sifted powdered sugar, 1 egg yolk, 1 teaspoon vanilla, ¼ teaspoon ground cinnamon, ⅛ teaspoon salt, and ⅛ teaspoon ground cloves. Beat until fluffy. Beat in as much of ¾ cup all-purpose flour as you can with a mixer. Stir in any remaining flour. Wrap dough in plastic wrap or waxed paper; chill 1 hour or until dough is easy to handle.

Plain Butter Dough: In a medium mixing bowl beat ½ cup softened butter with an electric mixer on medium to high speed for 30 seconds. Add ½ cup sifted powdered sugar, 1 egg yolk, 1 teaspoon vanilla, and ⅛ teaspoon salt. Beat until fluffy. Beat in as much of 1¼ cups all-purpose flour as you can with a mixer. Stir in any remaining flour. Wrap dough in plastic wrap or waxed paper; chill about 1 hour or until dough is easy to handle.

Nutrition facts per cookie: 173 cal., 10 g total fat (6 g sat. fat), 46 mg chol., 141 mg sodium, 20 g carbo., 0 g fiber, 2 g pro.

These naturally pretty cookies require no more packaging than bundling in a basket tied with an elegant ribbon. Try using a beautiful paper doily or hand-torn piece of art paper as a basket-liner—and add a few interesting-shaped cutters along with the recipe for the tarts. An antique European-style Christmas card featuring Father Christmas is a fitting gift tag.

kipfel

These rich cookies from the former Yugoslavia have two attributes much-beloved in Eastern European cooking and baking: the use of sour cream in the pastry dough and a plump, dumplinglike shape.

Prep: 35 minutes   **Bake:** 10 to 12 minutes

ingredients

½ cup butter

2 cups all-purpose flour

¼ cup granulated sugar

2 egg yolks

½ cup dairy sour cream

2 egg whites

1¼ cups ground nuts

½ cup granulated sugar

1 tablespoon lemon juice

¾ teaspoon ground
   cinnamon

   Sifted powdered sugar

   Ground cinnamon

1. For pastry, in a medium mixing bowl cut butter into flour until mixture resembles coarse crumbs. Stir in the ¼ cup granulated sugar. Make a well in the center. Combine egg yolks and sour cream. Add to flour mixture. Stir until mixture forms a ball.

2. Divide dough in half. Keeping half of the dough tightly covered, on a lightly floured surface, roll other half of dough to ¹⁄₁₆-inch thickness. Cut into 4-inch rounds.

3. For filling, beat egg whites slightly. Add ground nuts, the ½ cup granulated sugar, lemon juice, and cinnamon. Spread a rounded teaspoon of filling onto each round to within ¼ inch of edge. Roll up jelly-roll style; with seam sides down, press ends with tines of a fork to seal. Place on an ungreased cookie sheet, seam sides down.

4. Bake in a 375° oven for 10 to 12 minutes or until lightly browned. Transfer cookies to a wire rack; cool. Sprinkle with a mixture of powdered sugar and cinnamon. Makes about 30 cookies.

Nutrition facts per cookie: 120 cal., 7 g total fat (3 g sat. fat), 24 mg chol., 38 mg sodium, 12 g carbo., 0 g fiber, 2 g pro.

pepparkakor

Christmas in Sweden just might not arrive without these highly spiced cookies cut in the shapes of gingerbread men, hearts, and the much-beloved Christmas pig. In their country of origin, they are rolled thin.

Prep: 1½ hours   Chill: 2 to 24 hours   Bake: 5 to 6 minutes

1. In a medium saucepan combine sugar, molasses, shortening, and butter. Bring to boiling; reduce heat. Cook and stir for 2 minutes more. Remove from heat; cool for 45 minutes.

2. Add egg, cinnamon, orange peel, allspice, nutmeg, salt, baking soda, cardamom, and cloves to saucepan, stirring well to mix. Add flour, one-third at a time, stirring well after each addition.

3. Divide dough in half. Wrap and chill dough for 2 to 24 hours or until firm enough to handle.

4. Lightly grease a cookie sheet; set aside.

5. On a well-floured surface, roll half of the dough at a time to ⅛-inch thickness. Using a 3- to 5-inch cookie cutter, cut into desired shapes. If desired, make a small heart cutout in the center of larger gingerbread men. Place on prepared

cookie sheet. If desired, top with nuts, pressing lightly.

6. Bake in a 375° oven for 5 to 6 minutes or until edges are lightly browned. Transfer cookies to a wire rack; cool. If desired, spread cooled cookies with thinned Royal Icing. Makes 64 (3-inch) or 24 (5-inch) cookies.

Nutrition facts per 5-inch cookie: 132 cal., 4 g total fat (2 g sat. fat), 14 mg chol., 59 mg sodium, 22 g carbo., 0 g fiber, 2 g pro.

ingredients

½ cup sugar

½ cup mild-flavored molasses

¼ cup shortening

¼ cup butter

1 beaten egg

1 teaspoon ground cinnamon

½ teaspoon finely shredded orange peel

½ teaspoon ground allspice

½ teaspoon ground nutmeg

¼ teaspoon salt

¼ teaspoon baking soda

¼ teaspoon ground cardamom

¼ teaspoon ground cloves

2½ cups all-purpose flour

Finely chopped, slivered, or sliced nuts (optional)

½ recipe Royal Icing (see recipe, page 16), thinned (optional)

Serve up oversize cookies such as the intricately molded Speculaas on beautiful glazed ceramic trays that have similar dimensions. Pricing tags—found at business supply stores—make fun and innovative gift tags. Wrap the treats in cellophane for freshness, then in pleated paper wound with colorful ribbon and topped off by a smaller cookie to serve as a decorative and edible bow.

speculaas

To Americans, these traditional spice cookies most often come in the shape of a windmill. In Germany, Holland, Belgium, and Denmark, they come in many shapes made by using carved wooden cookie boards.

Prep: 45 minutes   **Chill:** 1 hour   **Bake:** 8 to 10 minutes

1. In a large mixing bowl beat butter with an electric mixer on medium to high speed for 30 seconds. Add brown sugar, cinnamon, baking powder, nutmeg, cloves, and salt. Beat until combined, scraping sides of bowl occasionally. Beat in egg yolk and milk. Beat in as much of the flour as you can with the mixer. Using a wooden spoon, stir in any remaining flour and, if desired, the almonds.

2. Divide dough in half. Cover and chill about 1 hour or until dough is easy to handle.

3. Lightly grease a cookie sheet; set aside.

4. Press a small amount of dough into a lightly oiled cookie mold. Unmold onto prepared cookie sheet. If cookie does not unmold easily, see "Every Nook and Cranny," below. Repeat with remaining dough. (Or, on a lightly floured surface, roll one portion of the dough at a time to ⅛-inch thickness. Using 2-inch cookie cutters, cut into desired shapes.) Place cookies 1 inch apart on the prepared cookie sheet.

5. Bake in a 350° oven for 8 to 10 minutes or until edges are golden. Cool on cookie sheet on a wire rack for 1 minute. Transfer cookies to a wire rack; cool. Makes about 48 (2- to 2½-inch) or 6 (8-inch) cookies.

Nutrition facts per 2- to 2½-inch cookie: 40 cal., 2 g total fat (1 g sat. fat), 10 mg chol., 30 mg sodium, 5 g carbo., 0 g fiber, 0 g pro.

ingredients

½ cup butter

¾ cup packed brown sugar

¾ teaspoon ground cinnamon

½ teaspoon baking powder

¼ teaspoon ground nutmeg

¼ teaspoon ground cloves

⅛ teaspoon salt

1 egg yolk

1 tablespoon milk

1⅓ cups all-purpose flour

3 tablespoons finely chopped blanched almonds (optional)

every nook and cranny

Some cookies, such as Speculaas, derive their characteristic shapes from specially designed molds. Look for cookie molds in specialty shops or mail-order catalogs. Before pressing dough into a mold, brush the mold lightly with cooking oil, paying particular attention to all the nooks and crannies. If dough still sticks to the mold, sprinkle the oiled mold lightly with flour before adding more dough.

ghraybeh

Orange-flower or rose water lends a touch of the exotic to these aromatic butter cookies whose origins lie in the Middle East, where they're often a Christmastime companion to pistachios and tangerines.

Prep: 30 minutes   Bake: 12 to 15 minutes

ingredients

1 cup butter

2 cups all-purpose flour

1 cup sifted powdered
    sugar

2 tablespoons milk

1 tablespoon orange-flower
    water, rose water, or
    1 teaspoon vanilla

12 blanched almonds,
    halved lengthwise
    and toasted

1. To clarify the butter, in a small saucepan melt it slowly without stirring. Skim off the solids that float to the surface. Pour the clarified butter into a measuring cup, discarding the milky liquid in bottom of pan. You should have about ¾ cup.

2. In a mixing bowl stir together the clarified butter, flour, powdered sugar, milk, and orange-flower water, rose water, or vanilla.

3. Divide dough in half. Divide each half into 12 small portions. Form small portions into ½-inch-thick ropes about 5 inches long. Form into S, X, or O shapes. Place on an ungreased cookie sheet. Place an almond half on top of each shape.

4. Bake in a 325° oven for 12 to 15 minutes or until the bottoms are lightly browned. Transfer cookies to a wire rack; cool. Makes about 24 cookies.

Nutrition facts per cookie: 125 cal., 8 g total fat (5 g sat. fat), 21 mg chol., 78 mg sodium, 12 g carbo., 0 g fiber, 1 g pro.

kourabiedes

During Christmastime in their native Greece, each of these almond cookies is crowned with a whole clove to symbolize the spices brought to the Christ child by the three wise men.

Prep: 40 minutes   Bake: 15 to 20 minutes

1. In large mixing bowl beat butter with an electric mixer on medium to high speed for 30 seconds. Add the ⅔ cup powdered sugar and the baking powder. Beat until combined, scraping sides of bowl occasionally. Beat in egg yolk, brandy or orange juice, and vanilla until combined. Using a wooden spoon, stir in flour and almonds or walnuts.

2. Shape dough into 1-inch balls. Place on an ungreased cookie sheet. Insert the stem end of a whole clove in center of each cookie.

3. Bake in a 325° oven for 15 to 20 minutes or until bottoms are lightly browned. Transfer cookies to a wire rack; cool. Sprinkle with powdered sugar. Makes about 60 cookies.

Nutrition facts per cookie: 58 cal., 4 g total fat (2 g sat. fat), 12 mg chol., 34 mg sodium, 5 g carbo., 0 g fiber, 1 g pro.

ingredients

1 cup butter, softened

⅔ cup sifted powdered
    sugar

½ teaspoon baking powder

1 egg yolk

2 tablespoons brandy or
    orange juice

½ teaspoon vanilla

2¼ cups all-purpose flour

⅔ cup finely chopped
    almonds or walnuts

Whole cloves

Sifted powdered sugar

stroopwafels

ingredients

- 2 cups all-purpose flour
- 1 tablespoon baking powder
- 2 teaspoons ground cinnamon
- 3 eggs
- ¾ cup sugar
- ⅓ cup butter, melted and cooled
- 1½ teaspoons vanilla
- 1 recipe Caramel Filling

Dutch tradition calls for these oversize, caramel-filled cookies to be placed atop a cup of hot coffee or tea to warm up their soft, buttery filling and make them pleasingly gooey.

Start to finish: 1¼ hours

1. In a small bowl stir together flour, baking powder, and cinnamon; set aside.

2. In a medium mixing bowl beat eggs with an electric mixer on high speed about 4 minutes or until thick and lemon colored. With mixer on medium speed, gradually beat in sugar. Beat in butter and vanilla. Add flour mixture; beat on low speed until combined.

3. Heat an electric mini pizzelle iron (for 3-inch-diameter cookies) according to manufacturer's directions. Place a slightly rounded teaspoon of batter in center of grid. Close lid. Bake according to manufacturer's directions. Use a spatula to transfer cookie to a paper towel; cool. Repeat, making about 48 cookies.

4. Prepare Caramel Filling. Immediately spoon 1 to 2 teaspoons filling onto 24 of the cookies, quickly covering filling with a second cookie. Makes about 24 sandwich cookies.

Caramel Filling: Line a 9×5×3-inch loaf pan with foil. Lightly butter foil; set aside.

In a heavy 3-quart saucepan melt ½ cup butter over low heat. Add 1 cup plus 2 tablespoons packed brown sugar, ⅔ cup sweetened condensed milk (about half of a 14-ounce can), and ½ cup light-colored corn syrup; mix well. Cook and stir over medium-high heat until mixture boils. Clip a candy thermometer to side of pan. Reduce heat to medium; continue boiling at a moderate, steady rate, stirring frequently until thermometer registers 234°, soft-ball stage (about 8 minutes). Remove pan from heat; remove thermometer. Stir in ½ teaspoon vanilla. Use about 1 cup of the filling for cookies.

Pour remaining filling (about 1¼ cups) into prepared pan; cool. When firm, lift foil out of pan. Use a buttered knife to cut into squares. Wrap each caramel square in plastic wrap. If caramels are still slightly sticky, refrigerate them; store caramels in the refrigerator.

Nutrition facts per filled cookie: 142 cal., 5 g total fat (3 g sat. fat), 39 mg chol., 105 mg sodium, 22 g carbo., 0 g fiber, 2 g pro.

A thoughtfully handmade envelope of art paper folded in the shape of your choice makes a gift of Stroopwafels all the more fun. Wrap a cookie or two in a waxed paper bag before slipping them into the envelope. Tie the package closed with ribbon or cording.

zimtsterne

These unusual, nut-infused meringue-and-cinnamon star cutouts from Germany are a great way to use excess egg whites.

ingredients

2 egg whites

1½ cups almonds, toasted and ground

¾ cup hazelnuts (filberts), toasted and ground

2 tablespoons all-purpose flour

1 teaspoon ground cinnamon

¼ teaspoon ground nutmeg

1 cup granulated sugar

Powdered sugar

Prep: 30 minutes   **Stand:** 1 hour   **Bake:** 10 minutes

1. In a large mixing bowl let egg whites stand at room temperature for 30 minutes.

2. Grease a cookie sheet; set aside.

3. In a mixing bowl stir together almonds, hazelnuts, flour, cinnamon, and nutmeg. Beat egg whites with an electric mixer on medium speed until soft peaks form (tips curl). Gradually add granulated sugar, 1 tablespoon at a time, beating on high speed until stiff peaks form (tips stand straight) and sugar is almost dissolved. Fold nut mixture into beaten egg whites. Cover and let stand for 30 minutes to let nuts absorb moisture.

4. Sprinkle some powdered sugar lightly over work surface. Roll dough on surface to ¼-inch thickness. Using a floured 2- to 2½-inch star-shaped cookie cutter, cut out dough. Place cutouts about 1 inch apart on prepared cookie sheet.

5. Bake in 325° oven about 10 minutes or until lightly browned and crisp. Transfer cookies to a wire rack; cool. If desired, sprinkle lightly with additional powdered sugar. Makes about 32 cookies.

Nutrition facts per cookie: 81 cal., 5 g total fat (0 g sat. fat), 0 mg chol., 4 mg sodium, 9 g carbo., 1 g fiber, 2 g pro.

springerle

These beautifully molded cookies get the name Springerle (SHPRING-uhr-luh) from the German verb springen, *meaning "to jump or to spring," in reference to a traditional mold featuring a jumping horse.*

Prep: 1 hour   Stand: Overnight   Bake: 20 minutes

1. In a small bowl stir together flour and baking soda; set aside.

2. In a large mixing bowl beat eggs with an electric mixer on high speed about 15 minutes or until thick and lemon colored. Gradually add powdered sugar, beating on low speed until combined, then on high speed about 15 minutes more or until soft peaks form. Add oil of anise. Beat in as much of the flour mixture as you can with the mixer on low speed (dough will be thick). Using a wooden spoon, stir in any remaining flour mixture. Cover bowl tightly with plastic wrap and let stand about 15 minutes for easier handling.

3. Divide dough into thirds. Roll one portion at a time into an 8-inch square about ¼ inch thick (keep remaining dough covered). Let stand 1 minute. Lightly dust a springerle rolling pin or mold with flour; roll or press into dough to make a clear design.

4. Using a sharp knife, cut cookies apart. Place on lightly floured surface. Cover loosely with a clean towel and let stand overnight.

5. Grease and sprinkle a cookie sheet with 1½ to 2 teaspoons crushed anise seed. Brush excess flour from cookies. With your finger or a pastry brush, brush the bottom of each cookie lightly with cold water; place on cookie sheet.

6. Bake in a 300° oven about 20 minutes or until cookies are lightly browned. Transfer cookies to a wire rack; cool. Store in a tightly covered container at least 3 days before eating. Makes 72 (2×1½-inch) cookies.

Nutrition facts per cookie: 49 cal., 0 g total fat (0 g sat. fat), 12 mg chol., 21 mg sodium, 11 g carbo., 0 g fiber, 1 g pro.

ingredients

3½ cups all-purpose flour

1 teaspoon baking soda

4 eggs

1 16-ounce package powdered sugar, sifted (about 4¾ cups)

20 drops oil of anise (about ¼ teaspoon)

Crushed anise seed

Cold water

A wonderful picture frame
is always a welcome gift—
especially if it doubles as
a serving tray for a collection
of Christmas cookies. Wrap
up a dozen Ruiskakut and a
frame, then use the same cookie
cutter as a pattern to make a
coordinating gift tag.

ruiskakut

Rye flourishes in the cold northern countries such as Finland, where these cookies originated. Rye flour imparts Ruiskakut with a delightful nuttiness.

Prep: 30 minutes   Bake: 8 to 10 minutes

1. In a large mixing bowl beat butter with an electric mixer on medium to high speed for 30 seconds. Add the ⅔ cup granulated sugar and beat until combined, scraping sides of bowl occasionally. Beat in rye flour and all-purpose flour with mixer on low speed until mixture resembles fine crumbs. Add water, tossing mixture with a fork until dough is moistened. Gently knead the dough until a ball forms.

2. On a lightly floured surface, roll dough to ⅛-inch thickness. Using 2- and 3½-inch round cookie cutters with scalloped edges, cut out dough, rerolling scraps as necessary. Using a smaller round cookie cutter (about 1 inch), cut a hole in the center of each cookie. (If you'll be tying cookies together, cut a hole in larger cookies slightly above center.) Place on an ungreased cookie sheet. Using a fork, pierce each cutout all over. Sprinkle cookies with coarse sugars.

3. Bake in a 350° oven for 8 to 10 minutes or until cookies are firm and begin to brown on the edges. Carefully transfer cookies to a wire rack; cool. Makes about 24 pairs (1 large and 1 small) of cookies.

Nutrition facts per cookie pair: 140 cal., 8 g total fat (5 g sat. fat), 20 mg chol., 78 mg sodium, 17 g carbo., 1 g fiber, 1 g pro.

ingredients

- 1 cup butter, softened
- ⅔ cup granulated sugar
- 2 cups rye flour
- 1 cup all-purpose flour
- 3 tablespoons cold water
  Coarse green and white sugars

155

chocolate pizzelles

Italy's crisp, wafflelike pizzelle (peets-TSEH-leh) is one of the oldest cookie recipes known. Pizzelles are made with an intricately designed iron that can be either electric or one that is heated on the range top.

Prep: 20 minutes   Bake: about 2 minutes per cookie

ingredients

1½ cups toasted hazelnuts (filberts)

2¼ cups all-purpose flour

3 tablespoons unsweetened cocoa powder

1 tablespoon baking powder

3 eggs

1 cup granulated sugar

⅓ cup butter, melted and cooled

2 teaspoons vanilla

1 recipe Chocolate Glaze

1. Finely chop 1 cup of the hazelnuts; set aside.

2. Place remaining ½ cup hazelnuts in a blender container or food processor bowl. Cover and blend or process until very fine but dry and not oily.

3. In a medium mixing bowl stir together the ground hazelnuts, flour, cocoa powder, and baking powder; set aside.

4. In a large mixing bowl beat eggs with an electric mixer on high speed about 4 minutes or until thick and lemon colored. Gradually beat in sugar on medium speed. Beat in butter and vanilla. Add flour mixture, beating on low speed until combined.

5. Heat an electric pizzelle iron according to manufacturer's directions. (Or, heat a pizzelle iron on range top over medium heat until a drop of water sizzles on the grid. Reduce heat to medium-low.)

6. For each pizzelle, place a slightly rounded tablespoon of batter on pizzelle grid, slightly off-center toward the back. Close lid. Bake according to manufacturer's directions. (For a nonelectric iron, bake about 2 minutes or until golden brown, turning once.) Turn warm pizzelle onto a cutting board; cut in half or into quarters. Transfer pizzelles to a paper towel to cool. Repeat with remaining batter.

7. Dip the rounded edge of each pizzelle piece into Chocolate Glaze; dip into reserved chopped hazelnuts. Place on a wire rack until glaze is set. Makes 36 pizzelle halves.

Chocolate Glaze: In a small mixing bowl stir together 1½ cups sifted powdered sugar, 3 tablespoons unsweetened cocoa powder, and ½ teaspoon vanilla. Stir in enough milk (2 to 3 tablespoons) to make a glaze.

Nutrition facts per cookie half: 120 cal., 5 g total fat (1 g sat. fat), 22 mg chol., 54 mg sodium, 17 g carbo., 1 g fiber, 2 g pro.

lebkuchen

One of the most famous of all German cookies, spicy Lebkuchen *(honey cakes) were invented before sugar was available. Many recipes call for these cookies to mellow and soften several days before eating.*

Prep: 35 minutes   Chill: 3 hours   Bake: 8 to 10 minutes

1. In a small mixing bowl beat egg with an electric mixer on high speed about 1 minute. Add brown sugar; beat on medium speed until light and fluffy. Beat in molasses and honey.

2. In a large mixing bowl stir together flour, cinnamon, baking soda, cloves, ginger, and cardamom. Add beaten egg mixture. Using a wooden spoon, stir until combined (dough will be stiff). Stir in almonds and the ½ cup candied fruits and peels.

3. Divide dough in half. Cover and chill about 3 hours or until dough is easy to handle.

4. Lightly grease a cookie sheet; set aside. On a lightly floured surface, roll half of the dough at a time into a 12×8-inch rectangle. Cut into 2-inch squares. Place on prepared cookie sheet.

5. Bake in a 350° oven for 8 to 10 minutes or until lightly browned around edges. Cool on cookie sheet for 1 minute.

Transfer cookies to a wire rack. Brush warm cookies with Lemon Glaze. Garnish with candied fruit pieces. Allow glaze to thoroughly dry. Store cookies, tightly covered, overnight or up to 7 days to soften. Makes 48 cookies.

Lemon Glaze: In a small mixing bowl stir together 1½ cups sifted powdered sugar, 1 tablespoon melted butter, and 1 tablespoon lemon juice. Add enough water (about 3 to 4 teaspoons) to make of drizzling consistency.

Nutrition facts per cookie: 82 cal., 1 g total fat (0 g sat. fat), 5 mg chol., 19 mg sodium, 17 g carbo., 0 g fiber, 1 g pro.

ingredients

1 egg

¾ cup packed brown sugar

½ cup full-flavored molasses

⅓ cup honey

3 cups all-purpose flour

1 teaspoon ground cinnamon

½ teaspoon baking soda

½ teaspoon ground cloves

½ teaspoon ground ginger

¼ teaspoon ground cardamom

½ cup chopped almonds

½ cup finely chopped diced mixed candied fruits and peels

1 recipe Lemon Glaze Candied fruit

brandy snaps

ingredients

½ cup sugar

½ cup butter

⅓ cup golden syrup* or dark-colored corn syrup

¾ cup all-purpose flour

½ teaspoon ground ginger

1 tablespoon brandy

As synonymous with Christmas in England as Charles Dickens and plum pudding, these crisp, gingered cylindrical wafers require quick work in the rolling stage, but are well worth the effort.

Prep: 40 minutes   Bake: 9 to 10 minutes

1. Line a cookie sheet with foil. Lightly grease the foil; set aside.

2. In a medium saucepan combine sugar, butter, and golden syrup. Cook over low heat until butter is melted; remove from heat. Stir together flour and ginger; add to butter mixture, mixing well. Stir in brandy.

3. Drop batter by rounded measuring teaspoon 3 to 4 inches apart onto the prepared cookie sheet (bake only 2 or 3 cookies at a time).

4. Bake in a 350° oven for 9 to 10 minutes or until bubbly and golden brown. Cool cookies on the cookie sheet for 1 to 2 minutes. Quickly invert cookies onto a cookie sheet and wrap each cookie around the greased handle of a wooden spoon or a metal cone. When cookie is set, slide cookie off spoon or cone; cool on a wire rack. Repeat with remaining mixture. Makes about 30 cookies.

*Note: Golden syrup, popular in England, is available in specialty stores and larger supermarkets.

Nutrition facts per cookie: 62 cal., 3 g total fat (2 g sat. fat), 8 mg chol., 34 mg sodium, 8 g carbo., 0 g fiber, 0 g pro.

As delicate as glass itself, cone-shaped Brandy Snaps are beautiful arranged in a glass bowl among colorful glass-ball ornaments. For Christmas party favors, fill Brandy Snaps with tiny candies, tie with ribbon, and place one by each guest's plate. Or, for the cordials connoisseur, place several cookies—point side down—in a beautiful brandy snifter tied with a bow.

pfeffernuesse

ingredients

- ⅓ cup molasses
- ¼ cup butter
- 2 cups all-purpose flour
- ¼ cup packed brown sugar
- ¾ teaspoon ground cinnamon
- ½ teaspoon baking soda
- ¼ teaspoon ground cardamom
- ¼ teaspoon ground allspice
- ⅛ teaspoon pepper
- 1 beaten egg

These German "pepper nuts" do have pepper in them, but the name of this classic recipe refers to the pepper countries, those once-exotic lands from which the spices of pepper, cinnamon, cardamom, and allspice come.

Prep: 30 minutes   Chill: 1 hour   Bake: 10 minutes

1. In a large saucepan combine molasses and butter. Cook and stir over low heat until butter melts. Remove from heat. Pour into a large mixing bowl and cool to room temperature.

2. In medium mixing bowl stir together the flour, brown sugar, cinnamon, baking soda, cardamom, allspice, and pepper. Set aside.

3. Stir egg into molasses mixture. Gradually stir in flour mixture until combined, kneading in the last of the flour mixture by hand, if necessary.

4. Cover and chill about 1 hour or until dough is easy to handle.

5. Divide dough into 12 portions. On a lightly floured surface roll each portion of dough into a 10-inch rope. Cut ropes into ½-inch pieces. Place pieces ½ inch apart on an ungreased shallow baking pan.

6. Bake in a 350° oven about 10 minutes or until edges are firm and bottoms are lightly browned. Transfer cookies to paper towels; cool. Makes about 240 small cookies.

Nutrition facts per 10 small cookies: 73 cal., 2 g total fat (1 g sat. fat), 14 mg chol., 50 mg sodium, 12 g carbo., 0 g fiber, 1 g pro.

lemon tuiles

These light and lemony cookies may be named for the French roof tiles they resemble, but their airy, delicate texture could not be more different from that of their namesakes.

Prep: 45 minutes   Bake: 5 to 7 minutes

1. In a medium mixing bowl let egg whites stand at room temperature for 30 minutes.

2. Line a cookie sheet with foil or parchment paper. Lightly grease foil-lined cookie sheet; set aside. Combine butter, lemon peel, and lemon extract; set aside.

3. Beat egg whites with an electric mixer on medium speed until soft peaks form (tips curl). Gradually add sugar, beating on high speed until stiff peaks form (tips stand straight). Fold in about half of the flour. Gently stir in butter mixture. Fold in remaining flour until thoroughly combined.

4. For each cookie, drop a level tablespoon of batter onto the prepared cookie sheet (bake only 3 or 4 cookies at a time). Using the back of a spoon, spread batter into 3-inch circles.

5. Bake in a 375° oven for 5 to 7 minutes or until cookies are golden brown around edges. Using a wide spatula, immediately remove the cookies and drape in a single

layer over a standard-size rolling pin (place cookies with the side that was against the cookie sheet against the rolling pin). Cool cookies until they hold their shape; then carefully slide off rolling pin and cool completely on a wire rack. Makes about 24 cookies.

Nutrition facts per cookie: 43 cal., 2 g total fat (1 g sat. fat), 5 mg chol., 11 mg sodium, 6 g carbo., 0 g fiber, 1 g pro.

ingredients

- 2 egg whites
- ¼ cup butter, melted
- 2 teaspoons finely shredded lemon peel
- ¼ teaspoon lemon extract
- ½ cup sugar
- ½ cup all-purpose flour

161

SUGARPLUM SHORTCUTS

santa's whiskers

ingredients

¾ cup maraschino cherries, drained and finely chopped

⅓ recipe Trio Cookie Dough (see recipe, below right)

Few drops red food coloring (optional)

½ cup coconut

When holiday time is tight, use one dough to create three cookies (see photo, opposite). Turn one portion of Trio Cookie Dough into a polka-dotted cherry treat complete with coconut "whiskers."

Prep: 25 minutes   **Chill:** 4 hours   **Bake:** 8 to 10 minutes

1. Pat cherries dry with paper towels. In a medium mixing bowl combine the the cherries, cookie dough, and, if desired, food coloring. Using a wooden spoon, mix until thoroughly combined.

2. Shape dough into a 10-inch-long roll. Roll dough in coconut until covered. Wrap in plastic wrap or waxed paper. Chill in the refrigerator for at least 4 hours or until firm.

3. Using a sharp knife, cut dough into ¼-inch-thick slices. Place slices 2 inches apart on an ungreased cookie sheet.

4. Bake in a 375° oven for 8 to 10 minutes or until edges are firm and bottoms are lightly browned. Transfer cookies to a wire rack; cool. Makes about 36 cookies.

Nutrition facts per cookie: 66 cal., 3 g total fat (2 g sat. fat), 8 mg chol., 25 mg sodium, 8 g carbo., 0 g fiber, 1 g pro.

---

trio cookie dough

ingredients

¾ cup butter, softened

¾ cup shortening

1½ cups sugar

¼ teaspoon baking soda

¼ teaspoon salt

1 egg

1 egg yolk

3 tablespoons milk

1½ teaspoons vanilla

4½ cups all-purpose flour

1. In a large mixing bowl beat butter and shortening with an electric mixer on medium to high speed for 30 seconds. Add sugar, baking soda, and salt. Beat until combined, scraping sides of bowl occasionally. Beat in the egg, egg yolk, milk, and vanilla. Beat in as much of the flour as you can with the mixer. Using a wooden spoon, stir in any remaining flour.

2. Divide dough into three equal portions. Use it to make Santa's Whiskers (above), Chocolate-Mint Thumbprints (page 166), and Lemon-Almond Tea Cookies (page 167).

Santa won't be disappointed with this cookie trio on his plate, and neither will anyone else. To give as a gift, individually wrap a sampling of Santa's Whiskers, Chocolate-Mint Thumbprints, and Lemon-Almond Tea Cookies and tuck them into a colorful stocking cap—or present them in a tin wrapped up with a winter-scarf bow.

chocolate-mint thumbprints

ingredients

⅓ recipe Trio Cookie
  Dough (see recipe,
  page 164)

2 ounces semisweet
  chocolate, melted and
  cooled

2 teaspoons milk

1 recipe Peppermint Filling

¼ cup chopped candy canes
  or hard peppermint
  candies

A cooling, crisp-as-the-winter-air mint filling tops off these soft, rich, chocolate cookies.

Prep: 25 minutes   Chill: 1 hour   Bake: 8 to 10 minutes

1. In a medium mixing bowl combine the cookie dough, chocolate, and the 2 teaspoons milk. Mix until thoroughly combined.

2. Shape dough into an 8-inch-long roll. Wrap in plastic wrap or waxed paper wrap. Chill in the refrigerator for at least 1 hour.

3. Using a sharp knife, cut dough into ¾-inch-thick slices. Cut each slice into quarters and roll each quarter into a ball. Place balls 2 inches apart on an ungreased cookie sheet. Press down in center of each ball with your thumb.

4. Bake in a 375° oven for 8 to 10 minutes or until tops look dry. Transfer cookies to a wire rack; cool.

5. Spoon a scant teaspoon of Peppermint Filling into the center of each cookie. Sprinkle cookies with the chopped candy. Makes about 48 cookies.

Peppermint Filling: In a small mixing bowl beat ¼ cup butter with an electric mixer on medium to high speed about 30 seconds or until softened. Gradually add 1 cup sifted powdered sugar, beating until combined. Beat in 2 tablespoons milk, ¼ teaspoon peppermint extract, and a few drops of red or green food coloring, if desired. Gradually beat in 1 cup sifted powdered sugar until smooth.

Nutrition facts per cookie: 74 cal., 3 g total fat (2 g sat. fat), 8 mg chol., 27 mg sodium, 11 g carbo., 0 g fiber, 1 g pro.

lemon-almond tea cookies

Paired with some simple finger sandwiches, these elegant little cookies make perfect fare for a holiday open house. Serve them with coffee, tea, or spiced warm cider.

Prep: 25 minutes   Chill: 4 hours   Bake: 8 to 10 minutes

1. In a medium mixing bowl combine the cookie dough, lemon peel, and almond extract. Using a wooden spoon, mix until thoroughly combined.

2. Shape dough into an 8-inch-long roll. Wrap in plastic wrap or waxed paper. Chill in the refrigerator for at least 4 hours.

3. Using a sharp knife, cut dough into ¼-inch-thick slices. Place slices 2 inches apart on an ungreased cookie sheet.

4. Bake in a 375° oven for 8 to 10 minutes or until edges are firm and bottoms are lightly browned. Transfer cookies to a wire rack; cool.

5. Spread about 1 teaspoon of the frosting atop each cookie. Sprinkle with sliced almonds. Makes 32 cookies.

Lemon Frosting: In a small mixing bowl beat ¼ cup butter, softened, with an electric mixer on medium to high speed about 30 seconds. Gradually add 1 cup sifted powdered sugar, beating until combined. Beat in 4 teaspoons milk, 1 teaspoon lemon juice, ¼ teaspoon vanilla, and a few drops almond extract. Gradually beat in 1 cup sifted powdered sugar until smooth.

Nutrition facts per cookie: 110 cal., 6 g total fat (2 g sat. fat), 12 mg chol., 40 mg sodium, 14 g carbo., 0 g fiber, 1 g pro.

ingredients

⅓ recipe Trio Cookie Dough (see recipe, page 164)

2 teaspoons finely shredded lemon peel

1 teaspoon almond extract

1 recipe Lemon Frosting

½ cup sliced almonds, toasted

No one will pass on this rich Italian version of fruitcake—Quick Panforte Bars—especially when it's packaged so prettily. For a pampering gift, wrap a couple of bars with a crossword puzzle book. Tie a pen and tea bag onto the bow as an invitation to linger over the puzzles—or over nothing in particular.

quick panforte bars

These rich bars are typical of traditional panforte—an Italian fruitcakelike pastry dense with nuts and candied fruit—in all but the preparation time.

Prep: 15 minutes   **Bake:** 30 minutes

1. Lightly grease a 9×9×2-inch baking pan; set aside.

2. In a large mixing bowl stir sugar cookie dough with a wooden spoon until soft. Add nuts, butterscotch or chocolate pieces, and, if using, dried fruit. Stir until well mixed. Pat dough evenly into the prepared pan. Sprinkle coconut over top, pressing in lightly.

3. Bake in a 350° oven about 30 minutes or until a wooden pick inserted near center comes out clean. Cool completely in pan on a wire rack. Cut into bars. Makes 32 bars.

Nutrition facts per bar: 109 cal., 6 g total fat (2 g sat. fat), 2 mg chol., 70 mg sodium, 13 g carbo., 0 g fiber, 2 g pro.

ingredients

- 1 18-ounce roll refrigerated sugar cookie dough
- 1 can (10 to 12 ounces) unsalted mixed nuts, coarsely chopped
- ½ cup butterscotch-flavored pieces or semisweet chocolate pieces
- ½ cup mixed dried fruit bits, coarsely chopped dried apricots, or golden raisins (optional)
- ½ cup shredded coconut

no-bake orange balls

ingredients

2 cups finely crushed, crisp unfrosted sugar cookies (about 8 ounces)

1 cup toasted hazelnuts (filberts), almonds, or pecans, finely chopped

1 cup sifted powdered sugar

¼ cup light-colored corn syrup

2 tablespoons orange, coffee, or almond liqueur

2 tablespoons butter, melted

Sifted powdered sugar (about ⅓ cup)

Swedish bakers make a confection of cookie crumbs moistened with liqueur or rum and wrapped in marzipan. Here, cookie crumbs are transformed into an elegant and easy shaped cookie studded with nuts.

Prep: 25 minutes   Stand: 2 hours

1. In a large mixing bowl combine crumbs, nuts, the 1 cup powdered sugar, corn syrup, desired liqueur, and butter; stir with a wooden spoon until well mixed.

2. Shape mixture into 1-inch balls. Roll in additional powdered sugar; cover. Let stand 2 hours. Roll balls again in powdered sugar before serving. Chill or freeze for longer storage. Makes about 40 cookies.

Nutrition facts per cookie: 69 cal., 3 g total fat (1 g sat. fat), 3 mg chol., 32 mg sodium, 9 g carbo., 0 g fiber, 1 g pro.

brown sugar bars

Homey bars or drop cookies can be made at a moment's notice when this three-in-one mix is on hand. Try these bars, Apricot Bars (page 172), or Cranberry Jumbles (page 173).

Prep: 10 minutes   Bake: 20 to 25 minutes

1. Grease an 11×7×1½-inch baking pan; set aside.

2. In a large mixing bowl beat together the eggs and milk; stir in the cookie mix until combined. Spread batter evenly in the prepared pan.

3. Bake in 350° oven for 10 minutes. Sprinkle chocolate pieces evenly over top of partially baked bars. Bake 10 to 15 minutes more or until golden brown and firm around edges. Cool in pan on a wire rack. Cut into bars. Makes 24 bars.

Nutrition facts per bar: 104 cal., 6 g total fat (1 g sat. fat), 19 mg chol., 35 mg sodium, 12 g carbo., 0 g fiber, 1 g pro.

ingredients

2   slightly beaten eggs

⅓   cup milk

2½   cups Brown Sugar Cookie Mix (see recipe, left)

½   cup miniature candy-coated semisweet or milk chocolate pieces

brown sugar cookie mix

ingredients

3   cups all-purpose flour

1   cup whole wheat flour

2   cups packed brown sugar

2   teaspoons baking powder

½   teaspoon baking soda

1½   cups shortening

1. In a very large mixing bowl stir together all-purpose flour, whole wheat flour, brown sugar, baking powder, and baking soda.

2. Cut in shortening until mixture resembles fine crumbs. Store tightly covered at room temperature for up to 3 weeks. To measure the mix, lightly spoon mix into a measuring cup and level with a spatula. Makes about 8½ cups mix.

apricot bars

ingredients

- 1 slightly beaten egg
- 1 tablespoon water
- ½ teaspoon vanilla
- 2 cups Brown Sugar Cookie Mix (see recipe, page 171)
- ¾ cup quick-cooking rolled oats
- 1 12-ounce can apricot (or desired flavor) cake and pastry filling or 1 cup apricot (or desired flavor) preserves
- ½ cup Brown Sugar Cookie Mix (see recipe, page 171)
- ¼ cup quick-cooking rolled oats
- ¼ teaspoon ground nutmeg or cardamom
- 1 recipe Lemon Icing (optional)

Flexibility is part of the fun of these soft, chewy cookies. Use apricot cake and pastry filling or apricot preserves in the middle layer, and flavor the crumbly oat topping with either nutmeg or cardamom.

Prep: 20 minutes   **Bake:** 25 minutes

1. Grease a 9×9×2-inch baking pan; set aside.

2. For crust, in a large mixing bowl combine egg, water, and vanilla. Stir in the 2 cups cookie mix and the ¾ cup oats. Spread mixture into the prepared pan.

3. Bake in a 350° oven for 10 minutes. Spread the partially baked crust with cake and pastry filling or preserves. In a medium bowl combine the ½ cup cookie mix, the ¼ cup oats, and nutmeg or cardamom. Sprinkle over filling. Bake about 15 minutes more or until top is golden brown. Cool in pan on a wire rack. If desired, drizzle with Lemon Icing. Cut into bars. Makes 24 bars.

Lemon Icing: In a small mixing bowl stir together ¾ cup sifted powdered sugar and enough lemon juice (3 to 4 teaspoons) to make icing of drizzling consistency.

Nutrition facts per bar: 127 cal., 4 g total fat (1 g sat. fat), 9 mg chol., 29 mg sodium, 21 g carbo., 1 g fiber, 1 g pro.

cranberry jumbles

Dried cranberries and almonds in the dough and a frosting flavored with fresh orange peel and orange juice turn the basic brown sugar cookie mix into a distinctive holiday-time treat.

Prep: 20 minutes   **Bake:** 12 to 14 minutes

1. In a large mixing bowl combine egg and cranberry juice or orange juice. Stir in the cookie mix, cranberries, almonds, and cinnamon.

2. Drop dough by rounded teaspoons 2 inches apart onto an ungreased cookie sheet.

3. Bake in a 350° oven for 12 to 14 minutes or until bottoms are lightly browned. Transfer cookies to a wire rack; cool. Drizzle Orange Frosting over tops of cookies. Makes 32 cookies.

Orange Frosting: In a small mixing bowl stir together 1 cup sifted powdered sugar, ½ teaspoon finely shredded orange peel, and enough orange juice (3 to 4 teaspoons) to make frosting of drizzling consistency.

Nutrition facts per cookie: 100 cal., 5 g total fat (1 g sat. fat), 7 mg chol., 19 mg sodium, 14 g carbo., 1 g fiber, 1 g pro.

ingredients

- 1 slightly beaten egg
- 2 tablespoons cranberry juice or orange juice
- 3 cups Brown Sugar Cookie Mix (see recipe, page 171)
- 1 cup dried cranberries
- ½ cup slivered almonds
- ½ teaspoon ground cinnamon
- 1 recipe Orange Frosting

For treats to go, place Simple Fudge Tarts in small paper bake cups and nestle them into a nut-filled box. Or, fill a small muffin tin with paper bake cups and place a tart in every other compartment. Fill the remaining compartments with the recipient's favorite nuts.

simple fudge tarts

Refrigerated peanut butter cookie dough serves as a shortcut crust for these small-in-size, rich-in-taste, three-ingredient tarts.

Prep: 20 minutes   Bake: 11 minutes

1. Spray twenty-four 1¾-inch muffin cups with nonstick coating; set aside.

2. For tart shells, cut cookie dough into 6 equal pieces. Cut each piece into 4 equal slices. Place each slice of dough in a prepared cup.

3. Bake in a 350° oven for 9 minutes or until edges are lightly browned and dough is slightly firm but not set. Remove tart shells from oven. Gently press a shallow indentation in each tart shell with the back of a round ½ teaspoon measuring spoon.

4. Bake 2 minutes more or until the edges of tart shells are firm and light golden brown. Let tart shells cool in cups on a wire rack for 15 minutes. Carefully remove tart shells from cups. Cool completely on wire racks.

5. For filling, in a small saucepan combine chocolate pieces and sweetened condensed milk. Cook and stir over medium heat until chocolate is melted. Spoon a slightly rounded teaspoon of filling into each cooled tart shell. Cool, allowing filling to set. Makes 24 tarts.

Nutrition facts per cookie: 75 cal., 4 g total fat (1 g sat. fat), 4 mg chol., 46 mg sodium, 10 g carbo., 0 g fiber, 1 g pro.

ingredients

Nonstick spray coating

½ of an 18-ounce roll refrigerated peanut butter cookie dough

½ cup semisweet chocolate pieces

¼ cup sweetened condensed milk

cherry-coconut drops

ingredients

1 7-ounce package
   (2⅔ cups) flaked
   coconut

2 tablespoons cornstarch

½ cup sweetened condensed
   milk

1 teaspoon vanilla

½ cup chopped red and/or
   green candied cherries

Looking like colorful Christmas lights encased in freshly fallen snow, these moist cookies are as festive and fun to look at as they are to eat.

Prep: 20 minutes   Bake: 12 to 15 minutes

1. Grease and flour a cookie sheet; set aside.

2. In a medium mixing bowl combine coconut and cornstarch. Stir in sweetened condensed milk and vanilla until mixture is combined. Stir in the chopped candied cherries.

3. Drop by small rounded teaspoonfuls about 1 inch apart on the prepared cookie sheet.

4. Bake in a 325° oven for 12 to 15 minutes or until lightly browned on bottoms. Cool on cookie sheet for 1 minute. Transfer cookies to a wire rack; cool. Makes about 24 cookies.

Nutrition facts per cookie: 71 cal., 3 g total fat (3 g sat. fat), 2 mg chol., 10 mg sodium, 10 g carbo., 1 g fiber, 1 g pro.

Decorative metal baskets make unusual vessels for these chewy coconut treats. For a fun stocking stuffer, stack Cherry-Coconut Drops, roll them up in cellophane, and tie the ends with colorful holiday shoelaces that can be worn long after the cookies are but a sweet memory.

nut wedges

ingredients

1 package piecrust mix
  (for 2 crusts)

¼ cup sugar

3 to 4 tablespoons water

1 cup finely chopped nuts

⅓ cup sugar

2 tablespoons honey

1 teaspoon ground
  cinnamon

1 teaspoon lemon juice
  Milk

½ cup semisweet
  chocolate pieces

1 teaspoon shortening

Here's the essence of that honeyed pastry-and-nut favorite baklava, without the hassle—and these have a chocolate topping.

Prep: 30 minutes   Bake: 15 to 20 minutes

1. In a medium mixing bowl stir together piecrust mix and the ¼ cup sugar. Add enough water to form ball. Divide dough in half.

2. On a floured surface, roll each half of the dough into a 9-inch circle. Transfer 1 circle to an ungreased cookie sheet.

3. For filling, combine the nuts, the ⅓ cup sugar, honey, cinnamon, and lemon juice. Spread over dough circle on cookie sheet. Top with remaining dough circle. Use tines of fork to seal edges and prick dough. Brush with milk.

4. Bake in a 375° oven for 15 to 20 minutes or until pastry starts to brown. Cool 10 minutes on a wire rack. While warm, cut into 16 to 20 wedges. Cool completely.

5. In a small saucepan combine the chocolate pieces and shortening. Cook and stir over low heat just until melted. Drizzle over wedges. Makes 16 to 20 wedges.

Nutrition facts per wedge: 214 cal., 13 g total fat (2 g sat. fat), 0 mg chol., 136 mg sodium, 24 g carbo., 1 g fiber, 3 g pro.

no-bake butterscotch treats

Instead of cutting these easy treats into traditional bars, sculpt the chilled mixture with an assortment of fancy cookie cutters—it'll look like you labored over them all day!

Prep: 20 minutes   **Chill:** 2 hours

1. In a large mixing bowl stir together melted butter, peanut butter, and powdered sugar. Stir in the crushed chocolate wafers. Press mixture into the bottom of an ungreased 13×9×2-inch baking pan.

2. In a heavy medium saucepan combine butterscotch pieces and whipping cream. Stir over low heat until pieces are just melted.

3. Carefully spoon and spread butterscotch mixture over crumb mixture. Sprinkle the chopped peanuts over butterscotch mixture.

4. Cover and chill at least 2 hours. Cut into bars or use 2-inch cookie cutters to cut out shapes. Store in refrigerator. Makes 48 cookies.

Nutrition facts per cookie: 130 cal., 8 g total fat (4 g sat. fat), 6 mg chol., 96 mg sodium, 13 g carbo., 0 g fiber, 2 g pro.

ingredients

 6 tablespoons butter, melted

 1 cup creamy peanut butter

1½ cups sifted powdered sugar

 1 9-ounce package chocolate wafers, crushed

 1 11-ounce package (about 2 cups) butterscotch-flavored pieces

¼ cup whipping cream

¾ cup chopped peanuts

puzzle pieces

ingredients

¼ cup all-purpose flour

1 18-ounce roll refrigerated
  sugar cookie dough

1 recipe Egg Yolk Paint

Give your kids' creative Christmas spirits a boost—let them make and give these delightful picture-puzzle cookies.

Prep: 20 minutes   Bake: Follow package directions

1. In a medium mixing bowl knead flour into sugar cookie dough. Divide dough into 6 portions.

2. On an ungreased cookie sheet, pat each portion of dough into a 5-inch square. Press a well-floured 3- to 4-inch cookie cutter into the center of the square. Carefully remove cookie cutter without removing dough. Using a table knife, cut outside portion of square into large puzzle pieces.

3. Brush dough puzzle pieces with different colors of Egg Yolk Paint.

4. Bake according to package directions or until bottoms of cookies just start to brown and centers are set. While still warm, carefully recut pieces with the cookie cutter and knife (an adult should do this step). Trim edges as needed. Transfer cookies to a wire rack; cool. Makes 6 puzzle cookies.

Egg Yolk Paint: In a small mixing bowl beat 2 egg yolks and 2 teaspoons water. Divide mixture among 3 or 4 small bowls. Add 2 or 3 drops of liquid food coloring or a small amount of paste food coloring in desired colors to each bowl; mix well. Apply with a small, clean paintbrush. If mixture thickens while standing, stir in water, one drop at a time.

Nutrition facts per whole cookie: 383 cal., 15 g total fat (5 g sat. fat), 84 mg chol., 359 mg sodium, 54 g carbo., 0 g fiber, 5 g pro.

A customized cookie puzzle makes an impressive and edible gift for kids of all ages. To give Puzzle Pieces in a style that fits their fun look, present them on a handmade decorative plate. Use a paper punch to make holes every $\frac{1}{2}$-inch around the edge of a brightly colored paper plate. Lace the holes with $\frac{1}{8}$-inch paper or fabric ribbon. Glue beads to the plate, if desired.

chocolate sandwich cookies

These cream-cheese-filled, chocolate-pastry wedges have an air of elegance about them, but with only five ingredients they go together beautifully.

Prep: 20 minutes   Bake: 10 minutes

ingredients

1   package piecrust mix
    (for 2 crusts)

½   cup sugar

¼   cup unsweetened cocoa
    powder

6   tablespoons water

1   8-ounce tub cream cheese
    with strawberries

1. In a medium mixing bowl combine piecrust mix, sugar, and cocoa powder. Mix well. Sprinkle 1 tablespoon of the water over part of the mixture; gently toss with a fork. Push moistened dough to the side of the bowl. Repeat moistening dough, using 1 tablespoon of the water at a time, until all the dough is moistened. Form dough into a ball. Divide dough into thirds.

2. On a floured surface, roll each portion of dough into a 6-inch circle about ¼ inch thick.

3. Cut each dough circle into 10 wedges; using a fork, prick dough in a decorative design. Transfer to 2 ungreased cookie sheets.

4. Bake in 375° oven about 10 minutes or just until set. Transfer pastry wedges to a wire rack; cool.

5. To assemble, spread about 2 teaspoons cream cheese over the bottom surface of half of the pastry wedges. Top with remaining wedges, bottom surface down, pressing together lightly. Store filled cookies in the refrigerator. Makes 15 sandwich cookies.

Nutrition facts per cookie: 188 cal., 11 g total fat (4 g sat. fat), 13 mg chol., 176 mg sodium, 20 g carbo., 0 g fiber, 2 g pro.

cereal wreaths

For a fun touch on these sweet no-bake wreaths, embellish them with a piped icing bow after they've firmed up.

Prep: 30 minutes

1. Line a large cookie sheet with foil or waxed paper; set aside.

2. In a large mixing bowl combine cornflakes, marshmallows, nuts, raisins, and cherries.

3. In a heavy medium saucepan melt candy coating over low heat, stirring often. Pour melted candy coating over cereal mixture. Stir gently until well coated.

4. Drop mixture by a ¼-cup measure onto the prepared cookie sheet. Flatten mixture slightly to form circles about 2 inches wide. Using the handle of a wooden spoon, make a ¾-inch hole in the center of each cookie, spreading the cookies to about 3 inches in diameter.) When cool, decorate with frosting, if desired. Makes about 15 cookies.

Nutrition facts per cookie: 234 cal., 11 g total fat (6 g sat. fat), 1 mg chol., 113 mg sodium, 33 g carbo., 1 g fiber, 3 g pro.

ingredients

4½ cups cornflakes

1 cup miniature marshmallows

⅓ cup chopped pecans or almonds

⅓ cup golden raisins

⅓ cup dried tart red cherries

1 pound vanilla-flavored candy coating, cut up

Purchased frosting (optional)

For whimsical party favors, use a straw to poke a hole in the center of each unbaked Peanut Butter and Chocolate Pinwheels slice. When baked and cooled, thread a few cookies onto the handle of a pinwheel. Secure the end with a licorice lace bow. Or, simply pack a dozen or so cookies in a tin filled with a mix of peanuts and an assortment of small wrapped chocolates.

peanut butter and chocolate pinwheels

If time is precious, cut the chilling step of these homemade slice-and-bake icebox cookies in half by stashing the dough logs in the freezer for about 30 minutes or until they're firm enough to slice.

Prep: 25 minutes   Chill: 1 hour   Bake: 8 to 10 minutes

1. In a large mixing bowl combine peanut butter cookie dough and flour; use a wooden spoon to mix well. Divide dough in half.

2. In another large mixing bowl combine sugar cookie dough and cocoa powder; use another wooden spoon to mix well. Divide dough in half.

3. Between pieces of waxed paper, roll out half of the peanut butter dough and half of the sugar cookie dough into 12×6-inch rectangles. Remove the top pieces of waxed paper. Invert one rectangle on top of the other; press down gently to seal. Remove top piece of waxed paper. Tightly roll up, jelly-roll style, starting from a long side. Repeat with remaining dough portions.

4. If desired, sprinkle half of the peanuts onto waxed paper. Roll 1 log of dough in peanuts. Wrap in waxed paper or plastic wrap. Repeat with remaining dough and peanuts, if desired. Chill dough logs 1 hour or until firm enough to slice.

5. Using a sharp knife, cut dough logs into ¼-inch-thick slices. Place slices 2 inches apart on an ungreased cookie sheet.

6. Bake in a 375° oven for 8 to 10 minutes or until edges are firm. Transfer cookies to a wire rack; cool. Makes about 60 cookies.

Nutrition facts per cookie: 77 cal., 4 g total fat (1 g sat. fat), 3 mg chol., 69 mg sodium, 10 g carbo., 0 g fiber, 1 g pro.

ingredients

- 1 18-ounce roll refrigerated peanut butter cookie dough
- ¼ cup all-purpose flour
- 1 18-ounce roll refrigerated sugar cookie dough
- ¼ cup unsweetened cocoa powder
- ½ cup finely chopped peanuts (optional)

salted peanut bars

Remember Salted Nut Rolls? One bite of these pleasingly sweet-and-salty treats will remind you of that perennially popular candy bar that comes in the familiar red wrapper.

Prep: 20 minutes   Bake: 25 minutes

ingredients

½ cup butter, melted

1 package 2-layer-size white or yellow cake mix

1 beaten egg

1 10-ounce package peanut butter-flavored pieces

1 cup chopped salted peanuts

2 cups miniature marshmallows

1. In a large mixing bowl stir melted butter into cake mix. Stir in the egg (dough will be stiff). Press dough into the bottom of an ungreased 13×9×2-inch baking pan. Sprinkle with peanut butter-flavored pieces and peanuts.

2. Bake in a 350° oven for 20 minutes or until edges are lightly browned.

3. Remove from oven. Sprinkle with marshmallows. Return to oven and bake 5 minutes more or until marshmallows are puffed and just starting to brown. Cool in pan on a wire rack for 1 hour. Cut into triangles or rectangles. Makes 32 bars.

Nutrition facts per bar: 175 cal., 9 g total fat (4 g sat. fat), 14 mg chol., 171 mg sodium, 21 g carbo., 1 g fiber, 4 g pro.

holiday snowmen

The simplest and sweetest way to decorate these kid-friendly snowmen cookies is with a glaze of powdered sugar icing, miniature chocolate chip eyes and buttons, and a gumdrop piece for a nose.

Prep: 30 minutes   **Bake:** 8 to 10 minutes

1. Cut cookie dough into 18 equal pieces. Divide each dough piece into 3 balls: one large (about 1¼ inches in diameter), one medium (about 1 inch in diameter), and one small (about ¾ inch in diameter). Assemble each set of balls ¼ inch apart in a snowman shape on an ungreased cookie sheet, placing the largest balls 2 inches apart so the snowmen don't bake together.

2. Bake in a 375° oven for 8 to 10 minutes or until edges are very lightly browned. Cool on cookie sheet for 3 minutes. Transfer cookies to a wire rack; cool.

3. For glaze, in a small mixing bowl stir together powdered sugar, vanilla, and 1 tablespoon of the milk. Stir in additional milk, 1 teaspoon at a time, to make glaze of drizzling consistency. Spoon glaze over snowmen. Decorate as desired with gumdrops and/or chocolate pieces. Makes 18 snowmen.

Nutrition facts per cookie: 148 cal., 6 g total fat (2 g sat. fat), 7 mg chol., 59 mg sodium, 23 g carbo., 0 g fiber, 1 g pro.

ingredients

1 18-ounce roll refrigerated chocolate chip, sugar, or peanut butter cookie dough

1 cup sifted powdered sugar

¼ teaspoon vanilla

1 to 2 tablespoons milk

   Gumdrops

   Miniature semisweet chocolate pieces

tree-topped brownies

ingredients

1 19- to 22-ounce package
   fudge brownie mix

20 holiday marshmallows
    or ½ cup (about 50)
    miniature
    marshmallows

Purchased frosting
(optional)

Nonpareils or other small
candies for decorating
(optional)

If the decorative holiday marshmallows shown here aren't available to you, these brownies also can be made with miniature marshmallows placed in an outline of a Christmas tree.

Prep: 15 minutes   Bake: Follow package directions

1. Grease a 13×9×2-inch baking pan (or use a foil pan for gift giving); set aside.

2. Prepare brownie mix according to package directions; spread into the prepared pan.

3. Bake as directed, adding holiday marshmallows in a tree shape the last 4 to 5 minutes of baking. Cool in pan on a wire rack. Decorate with frosting and nonpareils or other small candies, if desired. Cut into bars. Makes 36 bars.

Nutrition facts per bar: 107 cal., 5 g total fat (1 g sat. fat), 12 mg chol., 63 mg sodium, 16 g carbo., 0 g fiber, 1 g pro.

Baked in a toss-away tin, these impressive-looking brownies can simply be covered with plastic wrap and tied with a cheerful organdy bow for giving. As an extra touch, add a jar of fudge sauce and an ice cream scoop.

SWEETEN THE SCENE

victorian gingerbread house

This whimsical painted lady sweetly shows how the fancy embellishments on real Victorian houses came to be called "gingerbread trim."

ingredients

for 1 recipe gingerbread cookie dough

½ cup shortening

½ cup sugar

1 teaspoon baking powder

1 teaspoon ground ginger

½ teaspoon baking soda

½ teaspoon ground cinnamon

½ teaspoon ground cloves

½ cup molasses

1 egg

1 tablespoon vinegar

2½ cups all-purpose flour

• • • • • • • • • • • •

1 recipe Stained-Glass Window Panes

2 recipes Royal Icing (see recipe, page 194)

Assorted candies

Prepare the gingerbread cookie dough recipe twice, mixing each batch separately.

1. In a large mixing bowl beat shortening with an electric mixer on medium to high speed for 30 seconds. Add sugar, baking powder, ginger, baking soda, cinnamon, and cloves. Beat until combined, scraping sides of bowl occasionally. Beat in molasses, egg, and vinegar. Beat in as much of the flour as you can with mixer. Using a wooden spoon, stir in any remaining flour.

2. Cover and chill about 3 hours or until dough is easy to handle. Cut and bake as directed.

3. Enlarge the patterns on pages 220–221 as directed. If desired, cover both sides of pattern pieces with clear adhesive plastic to protect them. Lightly grease the back of a 15×10×1-inch baking pan. If desired, place the pan on a damp towel to prevent it from sliding around.

4. Roll some of the dough to ¼-inch thickness on greased pan. Place some pattern pieces 1 inch apart on dough. Cut

around patterns with a sharp knife. Remove excess dough (save for rerolling), leaving dough cutouts on pan. Cut out windows.

5. Bake in a 375° oven for 10 to 12 minutes or until edges are lightly browned and centers are just firm. Leaving warm, baked gingerbread on the pan, replace pattern pieces and trim edges exactly. Return gingerbread to oven and bake 3 minutes more or until very firm. Cool 3 minutes on pan. Loosen bottoms of gingerbread pieces with a spatula. Cool completely on pan. Transfer to wire racks. Repeat with remaining dough and pattern pieces. *If you allow gingerbread pieces to dry overnight, they will be even firmer and better for construction. Cover gingerbread pieces loosely with a towel.*

Stained-Glass Window Panes: Place about 60 hard clear candies of various colors in several rows ½ inch apart on a foil-lined baking sheet, mixing the colors. Bake in a 300° oven about 15 minutes or until completely melted into one large sheet. Remove from oven. With a long, sharp knife, immediately score hot candy into

victorian gingerbread house decorating and assembling

ingredients
for 1 recipe royal icing

- 3 tablespoons meringue powder
- 1/3 cup warm water
- 1 16-ounce package powdered sugar, sifted (about 4¾ cups)
- 1 teaspoon vanilla
- ½ teaspoon cream of tartar
- Paste food coloring

rectangles (see illustration, opposite top). You will need ten 3×1½-inch and two 3×2½-inch rectangles and one or two 2¼-inch squares. Let the scored candy cool completely. Peel off foil and break into pieces along scored lines. If desired, store several days in an airtight container, separating layers with waxed paper.

Royal Icing: In a large mixing bowl combine meringue powder, water, powdered sugar, vanilla, and cream of tartar. Beat with an electric mixer on low speed until combined; then beat on high speed for 7 to 10 minutes or until very stiff. When not using icing, keep bowl covered with plastic wrap to prevent icing from drying out; keep icing refrigerated until needed. Makes 3 cups.

to decorate and assemble house

Assemble and display the house on waxed paper on a tray or wooden cutting board that measures at least 16×12 inches. Pipe Royal Icing from a pastry bag fitted with a coupler and small star tip, or spread icing to use as "glue" to fasten pieces together. Experiment to find the right amount of icing to use. If you apply too little icing, the pieces won't stay together, yet too much icing takes too long to dry. Let each set of pieces stand about 1 hour or until the icing is dry before continuing.

1. Divide Royal Icing into smaller portions. Tint some of the portions with paste food coloring. Place some of each color in individual pastry bags fitted with couplers and decorating tips. If icing in a bag begins to dry and plugs the decorating tip, wipe tip with a wet cloth. The house shown was decorated with pink, white, blue, and violet Royal Icing using small round, small and medium star, and small rose decorating tips.

2. While gingerbread pieces are lying flat, decorate house sides and ends, bay window pieces, and entry front and entry porch roof with Royal Icing. When icing is dry, turn house pieces with window cutouts over onto crumpled paper towels to protect decorations. Attach stained-glass windows with icing. Let stand 2 hours or until dry.

3. Attach a house end to a house side, piping icing through a star tip or spreading a generous line of icing along edges to be joined. Press the pieces together, standing them on a tray or cutting board. Hold pieces in place with short beverage glasses, measuring cups, or heavy coffee mugs. Add remaining house side, then remaining house end. Keep supports in place until the icing has dried and house pieces are secure (at least 2 hours). Keep in a cool, dry location.

4. Attach a house roof piece along a house top edge; secure with straight pins until icing has dried. Repeat with remaining house roof piece. Let dry thoroughly. Remove pins.

5. Attach porch floor to assembled house. Assemble the entry porch front and sides with icing. When icing is dry, attach entry porch to the assembled house. Attach the entry porch roof.

6. Cut 6 candy canes into 3¼-inch-long pieces. Attach 4 of them to corners of the gazebo end of porch floor. (You may need extra hands or support objects to do this.) Pipe additional icing onto candy-cane tops and inner edge of gazebo roof support. While icing is still wet, place gazebo roof support on top of candy canes. Let icing dry slightly.

7. Attach the two end gazebo roof side pieces to house, piping icing on their edges and along edges of roof support (see illustration, middle). Let icing dry slightly; then add gazebo roof center pieces. To help support the points of the gazebo roof, place a gumdrop on top of gazebo roof support while icing dries. When gazebo roof is dry, attach center porch roof to gazebo roof and front door roof. Cut and attach candy canes beneath porch roof.

8. To make porch railings and other Victorian trims, place a piece of waxed paper over a sheet of graph paper or lined paper. Measure the distance between candy-cane poles. Using a small round or star tip, pipe porch railings in that size onto the waxed paper. In the same manner, pipe icing swirls, curls, and any other designs you want. Make extra trim pieces because some may break. Set aside to dry completely.

9. Attach bay window floor to end of assembled house. Attach the two bay window sides (see illustration, bottom) then the roof and bay window front.

10. To shingle the main house roof, generously spread some icing onto the bottom one-third of the roof. Press rows of hard candy rings into the wet icing. Repeat until roof is covered. To shingle gazebo roof, spread icing onto one section. Press jelly beans into icing. Repeat until roof is covered.

11. When railings and trims are dry, carefully peel them from the waxed paper and attach them to the assembled house. For a finishing touch, pipe icing onto all exposed cut edges of gingerbread. Add gumballs and tiny candies to roof peaks with dabs of icing.

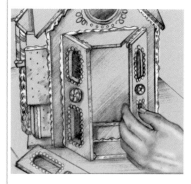

sugar cookie ornaments

ingredients

- 4 cups all-purpose flour
- 1 teaspoon baking powder
- ¾ teaspoon ground cardamom
- ½ teaspoon salt
- 1 cup butter
- 1 cup granulated sugar
- ⅔ cup light-colored corn syrup
- 1 tablespoon vanilla
- 1 beaten egg
- 1 recipe Royal Icing (see recipe, page 194)
- Paste food coloring
- Granulated sugar, colored sugar, and/or decorative candies
- Narrow ribbon or yarn

Add color, warmth, and dimension to your tree with these vanilla-scented cookie ornaments.

1. In a medium mixing bowl stir together flour, baking powder, cardamom, and salt; set aside. In a saucepan combine butter, the 1 cup granulated sugar, and corn syrup. Cook and stir over medium heat until butter is melted and sugar is dissolved. Pour into a large mixing bowl. Stir in vanilla. Cool 5 minutes.

2. Add egg; mix well. Add flour mixture to egg mixture; mix well. Divide dough into four portions. Cover and chill at least 2 hours or overnight. (If dough is chilled overnight, let it stand for 5 to 10 minutes at room temperature before rolling it out.)

3. For three-dimensional ornaments, on a lightly floured surface roll one portion of dough at a time to ⅛-inch thickness. Using a sharp knife, cookie cutters, or a fluted pastry wheel, cut dough into rounds, squares, diamonds, or heart shapes that are 3 to 4 inches wide. Make an even number of each shape, as you'll need to put them together later.

4. Arrange the shapes on an ungreased cookie sheet. Cut half of the cookies in half from top to bottom, but do not separate the two halves. Using a drinking straw, poke a hole off-center at the top of each whole cookie.

5. Bake in a 375° oven for 8 to 10 minutes or until edges are light brown. Carefully cut halved cookies apart. Transfer to a wire rack, keeping cookie pairs together; cool thoroughly. Prepare and tint Royal Icing with food coloring. Decorate cookies (wholes and halves) with icing. If desired, sprinkle wet icing with additional granulated sugar, colored sugar, or add decorative candies. Let icing dry.

6. To assemble, pipe icing onto cut edge of a cookie half; attach a cookie half to a whole cookie of the same size and shape. Let dry. Add icing and attach the matching cookie half to the other side of the whole cookie. (For easier handling, you may want to lean the fully assembled ornament against a cup.) Let dry completely. Run a ribbon or yarn through the hole of each cookie; tie into a loop large enough for hanging on a tree. Makes about 40 cookie ornaments.

gingerbread log cabin

What could be cozier this time of year than a cute little log cabin in the woods dusted with sparkling, sugary snow?

Prepare the gingerbread cookie dough recipe twice, mixing each batch separately.

1. In a large mixing bowl beat shortening with an electric mixer on medium to high speed for 30 seconds. Add sugar, ginger, cinnamon, and cloves. Beat until combined, scraping sides of bowl occasionally. Add egg, molasses, corn syrup, and water, beating until well combined. Beat in as much flour as you can with the mixer. Stir or knead in remaining flour.

2. On a lightly floured surface, shape one recipe of dough into ropes ½ inch in diameter. Cut ropes to make nine 9-inch logs, fourteen 7-inch logs, seven 3-inch logs, seven 4-inch logs, and twelve 1½-inch logs.

3. Place logs on ungreased baking sheets. With your finger, make a depression ½ inch from each end on all logs, except the 1½-inch logs. On the 1½-inch logs, make depression only in the center.

Reshape the depressions slightly to keep logs even in width.

4. Bake in a 375° oven for 8 minutes. Let cool on baking sheet for 1 minute. Transfer to a wire rack; cool completely.

5. Enlarge the roof, roof base, and gable pattern pieces on page 219 as directed. If desired, cover both sides of pattern pieces with clear adhesive plastic to protect them. Roll out remaining dough on the back of an ungreased 15×10×1-inch baking pan or flat baking sheet to ⅛- to ¼-inch thickness. (If desired, place pan or baking sheet on a damp towel to prevent it from sliding around.) Place pattern pieces 1 inch apart on dough. Cut around patterns with a sharp knife. Remove excess dough.

6. Bake in a 375° oven for 8 minutes or until edges are brown and dough is firm. Cool 1 minute on pan. Loosen bottoms of baked pieces with a spatula. Cool completely on pan.

ingredients
for 1 recipe gingerbread cookie dough

- 1 cup shortening
- 1 cup sugar
- 1 teaspoon ground ginger
- ¾ teaspoon ground cinnamon
- ½ teaspoon ground cloves
- 1 egg
- ½ cup molasses
- ⅓ cup corn syrup
- 1 tablespoon water
- 5 cups all-purpose flour

gingerbread log cabin decorating and assembling

decorations

1 recipe Royal Icing
(see recipe, page 194)

Cinnamon graham
cracker rectangles

Mixed nuts

Wheat wafers

Breadsticks

Small candies for
decorating

Powdered sugar
(optional)

to decorate and assemble log cabin

Assemble and display the log cabin on a large cutting board. Pipe Royal Icing from a pastry bag fitted with a small star tip or spread icing to fasten pieces together. Experiment to find the right amount of icing to use. If you apply too little icing, the pieces won't stay together, yet too much icing takes too long to dry. Let each set of pieces stand about 1 hour or until the icing is dry before continuing.

1. Prepare Royal Icing. Attach gables to roof base (see illustration, opposite top). Use custard cups to hold the gables in place while icing dries. Attach back roof to gables; set the front roof aside to attach later.

2. Assemble the log cabin walls using the 9-inch logs for the back, the 7-inch logs for the sides, the 3- and 4-inch logs for the front, and the 1½-inch logs for the door frame. To make the pieces fit together snugly, place the 7-inch logs that form the sides of the cabin and the 1½-inch logs that make the door frame rounded side up. Place the 9-inch logs that form the back and the 3- and 4-inch logs that form the front flat side up. Build the walls without frosting first to check the size of the logs and determine the assembly order.

Stack the walls 6 or 7 logs high. Use one or two 9-inch logs across top of front wall over the doorway. Once you're pleased, disassemble your log cabin; then reassemble it, piping icing between the logs to secure them (see illustration, opposite middle).

3. Attach the roof, then front roof piece, piping icing on tops of all 4 walls

4. To make the chimney, stack about 6 graham crackers, "gluing" them together with icing. Trim, if necessary, so they stand on a short edge under the roof on one side of cabin. Then stack 3 graham crackers together, fastening them with icing. Stand second stack on a short edge on top of the first stack; use icing to attach to roof gable (see illustration, opposite bottom). Cover a small part of chimney with icing. Place nuts in icing immediately. Repeat, adding icing and nuts until chimney is covered.

5. Attach wheat wafers to roof for shingles and breadsticks for roof peak.

6. Make as many windows as desired, decorating with icing. Attach breadsticks to porch corners and front corners of roof. Score breadsticks to the desired lengths with a knife; then snap to break.

7. Color some of the Royal Icing green and red. Use the colored icing to decorate the log cabin. Add a string of "lights" by piping red or green frosting along the edge of the house and adding small candies for lights. If desired, sift powdered sugar over roof or use some white icing to look like snow. Make icing icicles on the roof edges.

finishing touches

Add atmosphere and interest to your log cabin with these optional extras. Add as many as you wish.

Trees: Prepare cheery Green Cherry Trees (see recipe, page 13), making them larger or smaller as desired.

Barrels: Add icing bands to round, barrel-shaped root beer candies.

Wagon wheels: Pipe icing spokes and rims on purchased gingersnaps. Set next to cabin, if desired.

Butter churn: Attach a pretzel stick to a root beer candy with icing; add icing bands near top and bottom.

Fence: Break long pretzel sticks into desired lengths and assemble with icing.

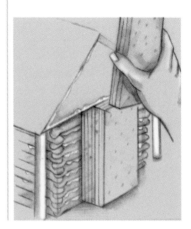

advent cookie tree

ingredients

1 recipe Special Sugar
   Cookie Cutouts (see
   recipe, page 26)
1 recipe Royal Icing
   (see recipe, page 194)
   Paste food coloring
   Colored sugar and/or
   small silver or gold
   decorative candies
   Thin satin ribbons

Count down to Christmas with this Advent tree hung with sugar-cookie cutouts artfully decorated with Royal Icing.

1. Prepare dough according to step 1 of the recipe. Divide the dough in half. Cover and chill dough about 1 hour or until dough is easy to handle.

2. On a lightly floured surface, roll half of the dough at a time to ⅛-inch thickness. Using a variety of 2½-inch Christmas cookie cutters, cut out dough. Place cutouts on an ungreased cookie sheet.

3. Bake in a 375° oven for 7 to 8 minutes or until edges are firm and bottoms are very lightly browned. Immediately after baking, use a drinking straw to make a hole in top of each cookie. Transfer cookies to a wire rack; cool.

4. Prepare Royal Icing and thin it with a little water just until it appears smooth when spread.

5. Divide icing and tint desired colors with paste food coloring. Place some of each color in a decorating bag (no couplers or tips are needed). Spread a base of white or colored icing over tops of cookies. (If desired, use an artist's paintbrush to apply the icing base.) Let icing base dry for 1 to 2 hours or until completely dry. Snip tips off decorating bags and pipe colored icing onto cookies. If desired, sprinkle colored sugar onto wet icing or press silver or gold decorative candies into icing. Let cookies dry 1 to 2 hours.

6. Carefully thread ribbons through holes in cookies and hang them on an ornament tree or on a natural branch as in the photo. If desired, store decorated cookies in the freezer and take out one cookie each day during Advent to hang on the tree or branch.

nativity scene

Be reminded of the reason for the season in the sweetest way with this manger scene made of sugar cookie cutouts.

1. In a medium mixing bowl beat shortening with an electric mixer on medium to high speed for 30 seconds. Add sugar, baking powder, ginger, baking soda, cinnamon, and cloves. Beat until combined, scraping sides of bowl occasionally. Beat in molasses, egg, and vinegar. Beat in as much of the flour as you can with mixer. Using a wooden spoon, stir in any remaining flour. Cover and chill about 3 hours or until dough is easy to handle.

2. Enlarge the patterns on page 224 as directed. If desired, cover both sides of pattern pieces with clear adhesive plastic to protect them. Lightly grease the back of a 15×10×1-inch baking pan. If desired, place the pan on a damp towel to prevent it from sliding around.

3. Roll some of the gingerbread cookie dough to ¼-inch thickness on the greased pan. Place pattern pieces 1 inch apart on dough. Cut around patterns with a sharp knife. Remove excess dough, leaving dough cutouts on pan.

4. Bake in a 375° oven for 10 to 12 minutes or until edges are lightly browned and centers are just firm. Leaving warm, baked gingerbread on the pan, replace pattern pieces and trim edges exactly. Return gingerbread to oven and bake 3 minutes more or until very firm. Cool 3 minutes on pan. Loosen bottoms of gingerbread pieces with a spatula. Cool completely on pan; transfer to wire racks. Repeat with remaining dough and patterns.

5. Follow directions in step 1 of Special Sugar Cookie Cutouts. Cover and chill, if necessary, until dough is easy to handle. On a lightly floured surface, roll to ⅛-inch thickness. Using cookie cutters in nativity and farm animal shapes, cut out dough. Place on an ungreased cookie sheet.

6. Bake in a 375° oven for 7 to 8 minutes or until edges are firm and bottoms are very lightly browned. Transfer cookies to a wire rack; cool.

ingredients
for gingerbread cookie dough

¼ cup shortening

¼ cup sugar

½ teaspoon baking powder

½ teaspoon ground ginger

¼ teaspoon baking soda

¼ teaspoon ground cinnamon

¼ teaspoon ground cloves

¼ cup molasses

½ egg or 2 tablespoons refrigerated or frozen egg product, thawed

1½ teaspoons vinegar

1¼ cups all-purpose flour

• • • • • • • • • • • •

½ recipe Special Sugar Cookie Cutouts (see recipe, page 26)

205

nativity scene
decorating and assembling

decorations

1 recipe Royal Icing
(see recipe, page 194)

Paste food coloring

Colored sugars and/or
sanding sugar

Flaked coconut

Liquid yellow food
coloring

Large pretzel sticks or
crisp breadsticks

Graham crackers

to decorate and assemble nativity scene

Assemble and display the nativity scene on waxed paper on a large tray or wooden cutting board. Pipe Royal Icing from a decorating bag (no couplers or tips are needed) or spread icing to fasten pieces together. Experiment to find the right amount of icing to use. If you apply too little icing, the pieces won't stay together, yet too much icing takes too long to dry. Let each set of pieces stand about 1 hour or until the icing is dry before continuing.

1. Prepare Royal Icing. Divide it into about 7 portions. Tint as desired with paste food coloring, leaving 1 portion white. (The scene shown uses blue, pink, green, yellow, ivory, and brown.) Place a small amount of each color in a decorating bag; set aside. Thin the remaining portions of icing until of spreading consistency.

2. Use thinned icing to frost the cutouts. If desired, use a small artist's paintbrush to paint multiple colors of icing. Let the icing dry thoroughly before adding detail trims. Snip the tips of the decorating bags filled with tinted icing. Pipe outlines and details onto cookies. While piped icing is still wet, immediately sprinkle colored sugar or sanding sugar onto icing. Shake off excess. Set cookies aside to dry.

3. For bales of straw, place coconut in a large plastic bag. Place several drops of yellow liquid food coloring in a ¼ teaspoon measure. Fill measure with water. Add to coconut in bag. Close bag and shake vigorously. With hands, gather yellow coconut into balls and mold into bale shapes. Cover until needed.

4. Attach two manger side walls to the back wall with icing; use glass measuring cups or heavy coffee mugs to hold pieces upright and steady until icing dries.

5. For the center vertical roof post, cut a large pretzel stick to 6½ inches. Prop the center post up using cups or mugs. For the roof beam, attach a whole large pretzel stick, resting one end on the post top and one on top of the back wall; let dry a few minutes. Beginning at front and alternating sides, lay large pretzel stick "logs" that stretch from the roof beam to the side walls (see illustration, top). The roof logs will have large spaces between them. If desired, attach some cut pretzels to front edges of gingerbread walls to

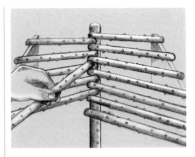

finish them. Attach a decorated star cookie with icing at top of roof.

6. When icing on cookie cutouts is dry, place cookies decorated side down on a work surface. Cut graham crackers into small triangles. Attach them at right angles near the bottoms of cookies for stands to keep the characters upright (see illustration, bottom). Let dry 1 or 2 hours before standing cookies up.

7. Arrange bales of straw, animals, and other cookie cutouts inside and around the manger. Add additional pretzels to look like wood pieces, if desired.

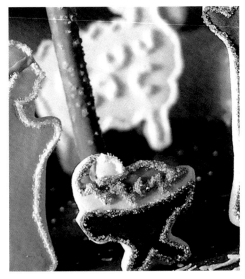

patchwork stockings and mittens

Hung from the tree, in a window, or given away as gifts, these colorful cream-cheese cookies shaped like mittens and stockings will warm hearts as surely as the real things warm fingers and toes.

ingredients

½ cup butter, softened

1 3-ounce package cream cheese, softened

1½ cups sifted powdered sugar

½ teaspoon baking powder

¼ teaspoon salt

1 egg

½ teaspoon vanilla

¼ teaspoon mint, peppermint, or almond extract (optional)

2¼ cups all-purpose flour Paste food coloring

1 recipe Powdered Sugar Icing

1. In a large mixing bowl beat butter and cream cheese with an electric mixer on medium to high speed for 30 seconds. Add powdered sugar, baking powder, and salt. Beat until combined, scraping sides of bowl occasionally. Beat in egg, vanilla, and, if desired, extract until combined. Beat in as much of the flour as you can with the mixer. Using a wooden spoon, stir in any remaining flour.

2. Divide dough into 5 portions. Place each portion in a bowl. Add food coloring (such as blue, pink, purple, and green) to 4 portions as desired, stirring until dough is evenly colored. Wrap each portion in waxed paper or plastic wrap. Chill about 1 hour or until dough is easy to handle.

3. On a lightly floured surface, roll each portion of dough to about ⅛-inch thickness. Using a floured 1-inch scalloped-edge square-, triangle-, or diamond-shaped cookie cutter, cut out dough. On an ungreased cookie sheet, arrange pieces in stocking and mitten shapes just larger than 3-inch cookie cutters, overlapping the edges slightly as needed (this may require 9 or 10 dough pieces). Using a floured 3-inch stocking- or mitten-shaped cutter, cut out dough. Remove scraps. (Reroll any scraps for cookies having a marble appearance.) Repeat with remaining dough pieces.

4. Bake in a 375° oven for 8 to 9 minutes or until edges are firm and bottoms are very lightly browned. Transfer cookies to a wire rack; cool.

5. Spoon Powdered Sugar Frosting into a decorating bag fitted with a small plain tip. Carefully pipe "stitch marks" around overlapping edges of shapes and edges of cookies. Makes about 18 cookies.

Powdered Sugar Icing: In a small mixing bowl stir together ½ cup sifted powdered sugar and enough milk (about 1½ teaspoons) to make icing of piping consistency.

fairy tale cottage

ingredients

for 1 recipe gingerbread cookie dough

½ cup butter, softened

½ cup shortening

1 cup sugar

1½ teaspoons ground ginger

1½ teaspoons ground allspice

1 teaspoon baking soda

½ teaspoon salt

1 egg

½ cup molasses

2 tablespoons lemon juice

3 cups all-purpose flour

1 cup whole wheat flour

• • • • • • • • • • • • •

1 recipe Sugar Cookie Dough

This bejeweled gingerbread cottage is where visions of sugarplums start. Be sure to make the recipe twice—don't double it—or the dough will be too difficult to handle. Use leftovers to make cookie cutouts.

Prepare gingerbread cookie dough recipe twice, mixing each batch separately. There will be some dough left to make cookies.

1. In a large mixing bowl beat the butter and shortening with an electric mixer on medium to high speed for 30 seconds. Add the sugar, ginger, allspice, baking soda, and salt. Beat until combined, scraping sides of bowl occasionally. Add the egg, molasses, and lemon juice and beat until combined. Beat in as much of the all-purpose flour as you can with the mixer. Using a wooden spoon, stir in any remaining all-purpose flour and the whole wheat flour.

2. Divide dough in half. Cover and chill about 3 hours or until dough is easy to handle.

3. Prepare Sugar Cookie Dough. Cover and chill about 2 hours or until dough is easy to handle. *After making the cottage, there also will be some Sugar Cookie Dough left to make cookie cutouts.*

4. Enlarge the patterns on pages 222–223 as directed. If desired, cover both sides of

pattern pieces with clear adhesive plastic to protect them. Using a floured rolling pin, roll out some of the cookie doughs to ¼-inch thickness on the back of an ungreased 15×10×1-inch baking pan, following Special Cutting Instructions on page 212. Place pattern pieces 1 inch apart on dough. Cut around patterns with a sharp knife. Remove excess dough (save for rerolling), leaving cutouts on pan.

5. Bake in a 375° oven for 10 to 12 minutes or until edges are lightly browned. Leaving warm, baked cookies on pan, replace patterns and trim away excess dough. (The more exactly the pieces are cut, the easier the house will fit together.) Let cookies cool completely on pan; then transfer to wire racks.

Sugar Cookie Dough: In a large mixing bowl beat 1½ cups butter with an electric mixer on medium to high speed for 30 seconds. Add 2 cups sugar and ¼ teaspoon baking soda. Beat until combined, scraping sides of bowl occasionally. Beat in 1 egg until combined. Beat in as much of 4 cups flour as you can with the mixer. Stir in any remaining flour.

fairy tale cottage decorating and assembling

decorations

2   recipes Royal Icing (see recipe, page 194)

Paste food coloring

Waffle-creme cookies

Fruit-flavored gummy circle candies

Tiny candy-coated tart candies

Multicolored nonpareils

Graham cracker squares

Honey-roasted peanut halves

Frosted bite-size shredded wheat biscuits

Peppermint candy sticks

Gumdrops

special cutting instructions

• Cut one roof piece B from sugar cookie dough; turn pattern over to cut a second roof piece from the sugar cookie dough. Use sugar cookie dough to cut 2 roof pieces from pattern A.

• Cut one end piece A from gingerbread dough for the middle of the house. For the tudor-style piece for front of house, cut pattern A on the dotted line. Roll out some gingerbread dough and some sugar cookie dough on a lightly floured surface. Cut the rectangular piece of pattern A from gingerbread dough. Cut the triangular piece of the pattern from sugar cookie dough. Place the 2 pieces on a lightly greased cookie sheet with long edges touching. Roll lightly to seal the seam. For the beams, cut ¼-inch-wide strips from scraps of gingerbread dough. Place the gingerbread strips on the sugar cookie dough end piece for tudor appearance (see illustration, opposite top).

• Using gingerbread dough, cut 2 sides from pattern A, 2 ends from pattern B, 2 sides from pattern B, and 3 chimney pieces from pattern B.

to decorate and assemble cottage

Assemble and display the cottage on waxed-paper-covered quilt batting set on a large tray or wooden cutting board. Pipe Royal Icing from a decorator bag fitted with small decorator tips, or spread icing to fasten pieces together. Experiment to find the right amount of icing to use. If you apply too little icing, the pieces won't stay together, yet too much icing takes too long to dry. Let pieces stand about 1 hour or until the icing is dry before continuing.

1. Prepare Royal Icing; tint as desired with paste food coloring. (The cottage shown uses white, yellow, red, and green icing.)

Using white icing, pipe on outline of windows on sides A and B. Pipe on door and door trims on tudor-style end piece A. Using yellow icing, fill in windows on house and door. Pipe on windowpanes. Fill in door with red icing. If desired, pipe Christmas light strings on tudor beams or use icing to attach colored candies to look like a string of lights.

2. Separate waffle-creme cookies into 2 layers. Attach one cookie layer by each window for a shutter. Attach fruit-flavored circle candies for wreaths by door and tiny tart candy pieces above windows. If desired, use green icing and a medium star tip to pipe a tree in one window; decorate

with nonpareils. Using red icing and the small round tip, pipe a bow on each shutter and wreath. For lights, pipe on icing and use a small round tip to pipe small dabs of red, green, blue, and yellow icing or add colored candy pieces to icing. Let icing dry thoroughly.

3. For porch, cut a graham cracker square in half lengthwise. Cut another square in half diagonally. Decorate a triangle as desired with frosting and nonpareils. (Discard remaining triangle.) Assemble the porch roof; attach it to tudor-style end piece A. Let icing dry thoroughly before assembling the cottage.

4. Working on a surface covered with quilt batting, pipe icing through a star tip to assemble section A, joining sides and ends. Press pieces together. Assemble section B

next to section A. Use a few dabs of icing to hold the end sections of A and B together. Use glass measuring cups or heavy coffee mugs to hold pieces upright and steady until icing dries thoroughly.

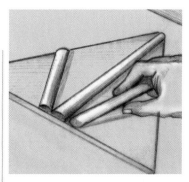

5. Using a star tip to pipe icing on edges of sides and end pieces of both sections of house, press roof pieces into position, placing the notched ends of roof sections B at the outside edge (see illustration, middle). This notched area allows room for the chimney.

6. Join the three chimney pieces with icing, making one thicker piece; attach chimney to end of house section B, fitting chimney into notched area of roof. Spread one area of chimney with icing. Place peanut halves in icing, allowing a little space between them so they'll look like stones (see illustration, bottom). Repeat until chimney is covered with icing and nuts. Let dry.

7. Spread part of a roof section generously with icing. Press frosted wheat biscuits into the frosting, staggering the rows like shingles. Attach peppermint sticks to peaks of both roof sections. Use peppermint sticks and icing to support porch roof.

8. Touch a star tip to edge of roof. Squeeze the decorator bag gently; then pull down to taper the frosting to a point. Pull the tip away. Repeat around all the edges of roof to make icicles. Add other candy trims.

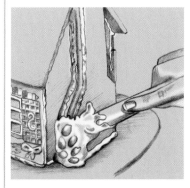

victorian cookie ornaments

These cornucopia-shaped cookies make lovely Christmas-party favors. Fill them with a tiny lady apple or with colorfully wrapped candies on the day of the party.

1. In a mixing bowl beat shortening with an electric mixer on medium to high speed for 30 seconds. Add sugar, baking powder, nutmeg, and salt. Beat until combined, scraping sides of bowl occasionally. Beat in egg, milk, orange peel, and vanilla. Beat in as much of the flour as you can with the mixer. Using a wooden spoon, stir in any remaining flour.

2. Divide dough into thirds. If necessary, cover and chill about 3 hours or until dough is easy to handle.

3. On a lightly floured surface, roll a portion of dough into a 9-inch circle. Trim to an 8-inch circle with a fluted pastry wheel. Cut into 8 pie-shaped wedges with pastry wheel. Carefully transfer to an ungreased cookie sheet, placing wedges about 1 inch apart. Using a drinking straw, make a hole about 1 inch from the bottom point. Make a hole about ¼ inch from the top corners, then another hole on each side midway between the top and bottom holes and about ¼ inch from sides (3 holes total on each side).

4. Bake in a 375° oven for 6 to 8 minutes or until edges are firm and bottoms are very lightly browned. Transfer cookies to a wire rack; cool. Repeat with remaining dough. Makes 24 cookies (enough for 8 ornaments).

5. Frost or decorate cookies with white Royal Icing, keeping holes clear. Use icing to attach small red candies. Let stand until icing has dried and candies are secure.

6. Once icing is dry, assemble the ornaments with the string or ribbon. Tie three 36-inch lengths of string together by making a knot about 4 inches from an end, then another knot 1 inch above that to form a tassel. Place 2 of the cookies together at a slight angle, matching up the holes. Starting from the bottom point of cookie, lace one long string from tassel through the holes in the two cookies. (Note: Use a large-eyed needle for lacing, if desired.) Run the lace through the top holes twice. Add a third cookie and lace it to the others. Bring the 3 strings together and tie a knot at the top to make a hanger. Hang by the top knot.

ingredients

½ cup shortening
¾ cup sugar
½ teaspoon baking powder
¼ teaspoon ground nutmeg
   Dash salt
1 egg
1 tablespoon milk
1 teaspoon finely shredded
   orange peel
½ teaspoon vanilla
2 cups all-purpose flour
1 recipe Royal Icing
   (see recipe, page 194)
   Small red candies
24 36-inch lengths white
   string or narrow
   ribbon

bargello

ingredients

- 1 cup butter, softened
- 1½ cups sugar
- 1½ teaspoons baking powder
- ½ teaspoon salt
- 1 egg
- 1 teaspoon vanilla
- 2½ cups all-purpose flour
- Paste food coloring

This cookie-cum-decoration takes its inspiration from bargello (pronounced with a soft 'g'), a traditional needlepoint design that produces colorful zigzag patterns.

1. In a large mixing bowl beat butter with an electric mixer on medium to high speed for 30 seconds. Add sugar, baking powder, and salt. Beat until combined, scraping sides of bowl occasionally. Beat in egg and vanilla. Beat in as much of the flour as you can with the mixer. Using a wooden spoon, stir in any remaining flour.

2. Divide cookie dough into 5 equal portions. Using paste colors, tint portions yellow, green, red, light green, and pink. Knead in food color, adding it slowly until dough is desired color. Divide each dough portion in half. Keep dough wrapped or covered with plastic wrap through all steps.

3. Break or cut two 10- to 12-inch lengths from ⅛-inch wooden dowel or skewers. Place dowels on a flat surface about 4 inches apart. Tape dowels to the surface at one end. Slide a piece of plastic wrap under the dowels. Tape the dowels' other ends to the surface.

4. Place 1 portion of dough at a time on plastic wrap between the dowels and flatten into a rectangle. Cover with another piece of plastic wrap. Roll dough to ⅛-inch thickness and about 6 to 7 inches long. To ensure uniform thickness, roll over the dowels, too. Between dough portions wipe dough from dowels, replace plastic wrap, and retape dowels as necessary. After each portion is rolled, wrap it in the sheet of plastic wrap and refrigerate on a cookie sheet.

5. Using a long, sharp knife, cut each portion of colored dough lengthwise into ⅛-inch-wide strips. Cover 2 cookie sheets with plastic wrap. Following the list of dough colors on page 218, set up 4 of Ribbon A on one sheet (start ribbons about 2 inches apart). On the other sheet set up 3 of Ribbon B and one of Ribbon C. Add the strips from left to right, placing them snugly next to each other and keeping one end fairly even. If a strip breaks, place it in position and press back together. The length of strips may be

bargello

different and can be trimmed later. Cover and chill ribbons. If dough portions begin to soften while cutting strips, cover and chill until firm again.

dough colors
Ribbon A—Light green, green, pink, yellow, red, yellow, pink, green.
Ribbon B—Green, light green, green, pink, yellow, red, yellow, pink.
Ribbon C—Pink, green, light green, green, pink, yellow, red, yellow.

6. To assemble a bargello square, carefully pick up a B ribbon and place it on top of an A ribbon, lining up the long edges. Top that, in order, with ribbons C, B, and A. Then top with another A ribbon, but rotate it so the light green strip rests on top of the green strip. Then add the remaining A (not rotated) and B ribbons. Gently pat the stacks together. Trim ends. Wrap in plastic wrap and freeze 1 to 2 hours or overnight, or until firm enough to slice. Repeat with remaining dough,

cutting more ⅛-inch strips. (There should be enough dough strips to make 3 stacks of ribbons.)

7. Cut chilled stacks into ⅛-inch-thick slices. Arrange the squares on an ungreased cookie sheet in sets of 4 in a pinwheel pattern, or in sets of 2, 3, or 4 in a line. Make holes for ribbon with a drinking straw, if desired.

8. Bake in a 350° oven about 7 minutes or until edges just begin to brown. Cool on cookie sheet for 1 minute. Transfer cookies to a wire rack; cool. Makes about 30 cookies.

Note: If you have any leftover dough, reroll any scraps to ⅛-inch thickness for cookies having a marble appearance. Cut into desired shapes, and bake as directed.

pattern: gingerbread log cabin (pages 198–201)

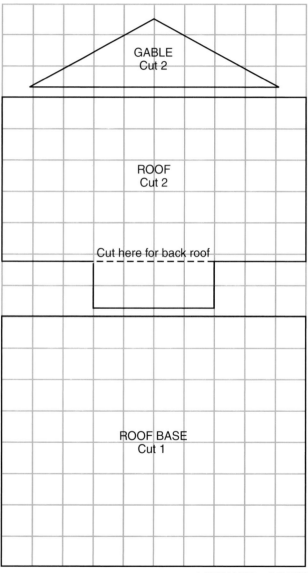

GABLE
Cut 2

ROOF
Cut 2

Cut here for back roof

ROOF BASE
Cut 1

1 SQUARE = 1 INCH

pattern: victorian gingerbread house (pages 192–195)

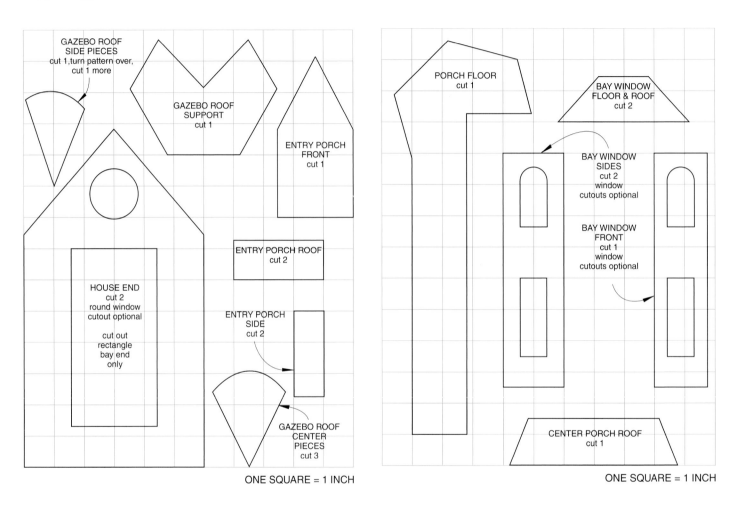

GAZEBO ROOF
SIDE PIECES
cut 1,turn pattern over,
cut 1 more

GAZEBO ROOF
SUPPORT
cut 1

ENTRY PORCH
FRONT
cut 1

HOUSE END
cut 2
round window
cutout optional

cut out
rectangle
bay end
only

ENTRY PORCH ROOF
cut 2

ENTRY PORCH
SIDE
cut 2

GAZEBO ROOF
CENTER
PIECES
cut 3

PORCH FLOOR
cut 1

BAY WINDOW
FLOOR & ROOF
cut 2

BAY WINDOW
SIDES
cut 2
window
cutouts optional

BAY WINDOW
FRONT
cut 1
window
cutouts optional

CENTER PORCH ROOF
cut 1

ONE SQUARE = 1 INCH

ONE SQUARE = 1 INCH

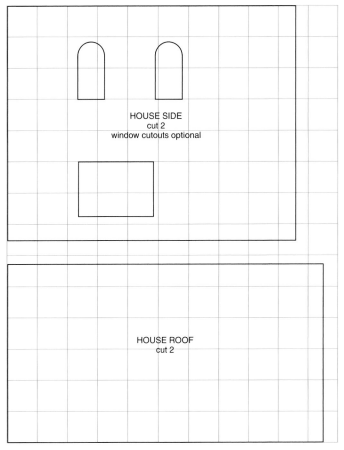

HOUSE SIDE
cut 2
window cutouts optional

HOUSE ROOF
cut 2

ONE SQUARE = 1 INCH

pattern: fairy tale cottage (pages 210–213)

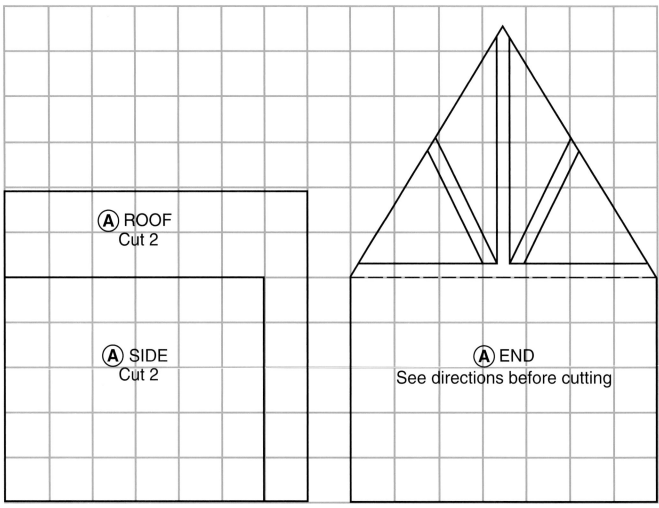

A) ROOF
Cut 2

A) SIDE
Cut 2

A) END
See directions before cutting

1 SQUARE = 1 INCH

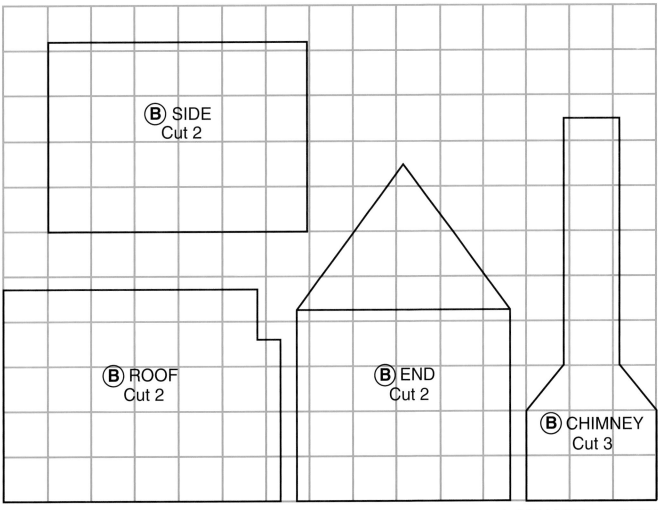

(B) SIDE
Cut 2

(B) ROOF
Cut 2

(B) END
Cut 2

(B) CHIMNEY
Cut 3

1 SQUARE = 1 INCH

223

pattern: nativity scene (pages 204–207)

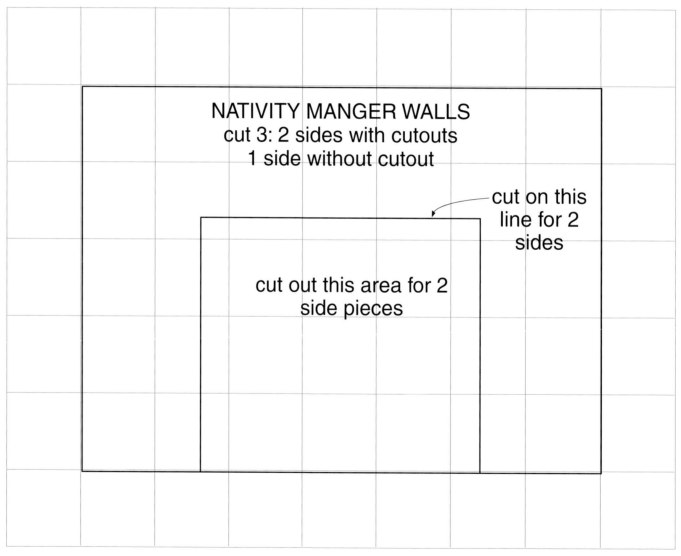

NATIVITY MANGER WALLS
cut 3: 2 sides with cutouts
1 side without cutout

cut on this line for 2 sides

cut out this area for 2 side pieces

1 SQUARE = 1 INCH

COOKIE
BASICS

OUTFITTING THE KITCHEN

Although baking Christmas cookies would be easier with a crew of elves for help, all you need are an electric mixer and a few everyday kitchen utensils.

■ *Electric Mixers.* Although mixing cookie dough is quite doable with either a portable (handheld) or a free-standing electric mixer, a free-standing mixer makes the job just a tad easier. Both types of mixers do an admirable job of mixing butter, sugar, and eggs, but with some portable mixers, you'll need to stir more of the flour in by hand.

■ *Utensils.* When equipping your kitchen for baking, it's easy to overlook humble wooden spoons and rubber scrapers, but these simple utensils are vital to mixing cookies. Because many cookie doughs are on the stiff side, purchase sturdy wooden spoons and scrapers. You'll also need a pancake turner for removing cookies from the cookie sheets.

■ *Pastry Cloth and Stocking.* For cutout cookies, rolling the dough out on a pastry cloth prevents it from sticking to the work surface. Slip a pastry stocking over the rolling pin, too. With a pastry cloth and stocking you'll avoid working additional flour into the dough, which toughens the cookies.

■ *Cookie Cutters, Molds, and Stamps.* Ardent cookie bakers collect cookie cutters, molds, and stamps with passion. Cookie cutters are readily available in grocery stores and kitchen stores. Some traditional cookies are shaped by pressing the dough into a mold, generally made of wood or a ceramic material. A cookie stamp can be used to press designs into balls of dough. In specialty kitchenware shops, keep your eye out for out-of-the-ordinary cookie cutters as well as cookie molds and stamps or check Sources on page 230.

■ *Bakeware.* Light-colored, dull-finished, heavy-gauge cookie

---

For Good Measure

Accuracy in measuring ingredients is critical to successful cookie baking. Here's how to measure the most common ingredients.

Flour. Stir the flour in the bag or canister to lighten it. Gently spoon flour into a dry measuring cup. Level it off the top with the straight side of a knife.

Granulated sugar. Spoon the sugar into a dry measuring cup. Level it off the top with the straight side of a knife.

Powdered sugar. Sift powdered sugar before measuring. Spoon into a dry measuring cup and level off the top.

Brown sugar. Spoon brown sugar into a measuring cup, packing it down with your hand or the back of a spoon as you add more; level off the top. When the measuring cup is turned over to remove the sugar, the packed brown sugar should hold its shape.

Butter and shortening. To measure sticks of butter or shortening, follow the markings on the wrapper. To measure unwrapped butter, soften it, and then use a rubber spatula to firmly press the butter into a dry measuring cup, removing any air bubbles. Level off the top with the straight edge of a knife. Measure shortening from cans the same way, except do not soften.

Liquids. Pour the liquid into a glass or clear plastic liquid measuring cup set on a level surface. Bend down so your eye is level with the marking on the cup.

sheets are best.

Old cookie sheets with darkened surfaces can cause overbrown cookie bottoms. Shiny cookie sheets are best for cookies that should not brown too much on the bottoms, such as shortbread. Nonstick cookies sheets are fine to use if you want to skip the greasing step. However, the dough may not spread as much, resulting in thicker cookies with smooth bottoms. Insulated cookie sheets may cause problems for cookies high in butter, shaped cookies, and some drop cookies because the butter may start to melt and leak out before the dough is set.

For best results with bar cookies, use sturdy single-wall aluminum baking pans or jelly-roll pans. Use the size of pan specified in the recipe or a substitution suggested in the tip on page 128.

■ *Cooling Racks.* You'll want several wire racks for cooling the cookies. The wire grids of the rack permit air to circulate freely around the cookies, preventing them from becoming soggy. Cooling racks placed over waxed paper are handy for drizzling cookies with melted chocolate or icing.

STOCKING THE PANTRY

Just like the instruments in an orchestra rendering Christmas carols, the ingredients that go into cookie dough work in harmony. Proper care and storage of the ingredients is the first step to perfect cookies.

■ *Eggs.* Purchase clean, fresh eggs from refrigerated display cases. At home, refrigerate them promptly in their original carton. Do not wash eggs before storing or using them, and discard eggs with cracked shells. For best quality, use raw eggs within one week of purchase, although they can be refrigerated safely for as long as five weeks. If you set out eggs before baking, be sure to use them within 2 hours. All of the recipes in this book were tested using large eggs.

■ *Fats.* Butter produces the richest, tenderest, and most flavorful cookies. Salted and unsalted butter can be used interchange- ably; however, if you use unsalted butter, you'll need to increase the amount of salt in the recipe (¼ teaspoon salt per ½ cup unsalted butter). Store butter in the refrigerator

Manage with Margarine

All of the recipes in this book call for butter rather than margarine. In cookies, butter gives a wonderful flavor and ensures the best results. Although cookies made with some margarines can be satisfactory, choosing the right margarine can be tricky.

Many margarines found at the supermarket today contain more water than oil, which will yield undesirable results. If you choose to use margarine instead of butter, select a stick margarine that contains at least 60 to 80 percent vegetable oil (oil content is listed on the package). Stick margarines will also produce a soft dough, so you may need to chill the dough longer than directed in the recipe or freeze the dough. Diet, whipped, liquid, and soft spreads or margarines are for table use—not for baking. Their high water content can cause cookie dough, as well as the baked cookies, to be wet and tough.

for up to one month or in the freezer for six to nine months.

Shortening is a solid fat that has been made from vegetable oil. It now comes packaged in sticks conveniently marked with tablespoon and cup measurements. Shortening can be stored at room temperature for up to a year. Plain and butter- flavored types are available; use whichever you prefer for baked products. If an icing recipe calls for shortening and you want the icing to be white, use plain shortening for a cleaner color.

■ *Sugars.* When a recipe calls for sugar, use white granulated sugar. Powdered sugar or confectioners' sugar refers to granulated sugar that has been pulverized; cornstarch is often added to prevent clumping. Sift powdered sugar before measuring. Brown sugar is a mix of granulated sugar and molasses; the amount of molasses determines whether the sugar is light or dark. If you purchase sugar in boxes, transfer it to a sealed plastic bag or an airtight container. When stored in a cool, dry place, sugars will keep indefinitely.

■ *Flours.* Most of the recipes in this cookbook use all-purpose flour, although a few may include

When it comes to melting chocolate, slow and steady wins the race. Chocolate burns easily, and when melted too quickly, it becomes grainy. To keep chocolate smooth and silky, follow these suggestions:

If using chocolate squares, coarsely chop them before melting. Put the chocolate in a heavy-bottomed saucepan over the lowest heat. Using a wooden spoon, stir constantly until the chocolate just begins to melt. Remove the saucepan from the heat and continue stirring until melted chocolate is smooth. If necessary, return to the heat for a few seconds.

To melt chocolate in a microwave, cook the chocolate, uncovered, only until it's soft. Stir it often to keep the heat evenly distributed.

some whole wheat flour. Store both types of flour in sealed plastic bags or transfer them to airtight storage containers and keep them in a cool, dry place. All-purpose flour will stay fresh 10 to 15 months; whole wheat flour will stay fresh up to 5 months.

■ **Leavenings.** Both baking powder and baking soda are important to baking, making cookies rise and become light. Store them in airtight containers in a cool, dry place. For best results, check the expiration date on the packages or replace them every 6 months.

■ **Chocolate.** Pure chocolate is the end product of roasting, shelling, and grinding cacao beans. About 50 percent of it is cocoa butter, a vegetable fat that gives chocolate its smooth-as-silk texture. In the grocery store chocolate is available in the following forms:
• Unsweetened chocolate is pure chocolate with no sugar or flavorings added. Extra cocoa butter and sugar are added to pure chocolate to produce bittersweet and semisweet chocolate. Bittersweet chocolate must contain at least 35 percent pure chocolate, while the amount of pure chocolate in semisweet chocolate can range from 15 to 35 percent.
• Unsweetened cocoa powder results from the grinding of the chocolate solids remaining after

most of the cocoa butter has been extracted from pure chocolate.
• White chocolate is not a true chocolate but a concoction of sugar, vegetable fat other than cocoa butter, dry milk solids, and flavorings. It's available in the form of white baking bars and pieces and white or tinted candy coatings.

DECORATING COOKIES

Deck the halls; trim the tree—Christmas is a time to decorate and make even the ordinary extraordinary. No wonder Christmas cookies adorned with swirls of frosting, sprinkles of sugar, and drizzles of chocolate grace treat platters everywhere. Each recipe in this cookbook includes instructions so you can make your cookies look just like the ones in the photos. Or, you can use the same techniques to dress up your own sugar cookie recipe.

■ *Frosting and Paint.* For simple decorations, pipe frosting using a disposable pastry bag and decorating tips. Just three decorating tips—writing, star, and small rose—will yield an endless number of trims.

Anyone can be a trim artist with unbaked cutout cookies and Egg Yolk Paint (see recipe, page 46). Use the paint to add colorful details to the cutout shapes. You'll need a few custard cups to mix the paint and several small, clean watercolor paintbrushes to apply it. Use a different brush for

Tinting cookie doughs and frostings shades of red, green, or other hues transforms plain-Jane cookies into gaily colored treats. Depending on the final product, either liquid or paste food colorings can do the job. Available in four colors (red, blue, green, and yellow), liquid food colorings are the easiest to find and the least costly. You can buy a package with a small bottle of each color or larger bottles of a single color. Liquid colorings work best for creating pastel doughs and icings. For a greater variety of colors and more intense color use paste food colorings. The dozens of shades are sold in sets or individually. Use a clean toothpick to add paste to dough or frosting. Be careful not to transfer dough or frosting into the paste or the paste will mold.

each color, and don't paint one color on top of another. Leave a small space of unpainted cookie between the colors so they don't run together.

■ *Sprinkles.* An easy way to give sparkle to cookies is to sprinkle them with pearl or coarse sugar or edible glitter. Check out mail-order catalogs or shops that specialize in cake decorating supplies for other products (see Sources on page 230). Look for additional decorative items, such as petal dust (a powdered food coloring that may be brushed on cookies or frosting) and nonpareils (tiny sugar balls).

■ *Chocolate.* Cookies drizzled or coated with chocolate are dressed for any occasion. Use a spoon to drizzle melted chocolate over the cookies or dip half of each cookie into melted chocolate (see "Melting Chocolate" on page 228). Garnish frosted bars with grated chocolate or chocolate curls.

MAKING COOKIES LAST

Follow these tips to ensure that your cookies stay in tip-top shape from the time you bake them until you serve them to friends and family members or set some out for St. Nick.

- If you aren't going to serve your cookies in the next three days, freeze them.
- Make sure cookies are completely cool before storing them. If they are still warm, they're likely to stick together.
- Store crisp and soft cookies separately. Stored together, they all become soft.
- Use tightly covered containers or sealed plastic bags.
- Store bar cookies in a tightly covered container or in their own baking pan, tightly covered with plastic wrap or foil.
- Any cookies with a filling or frosting that contains cream cheese or yogurt must be stored in the refrigerator.
- To restore moisture to soft cookies that have begun to dry out, wrap a wedge of apple or a slice of bread in waxed paper. Put it in the container with the cookies and seal.

Remove the apple or bread after 24 hours.
- To jump-start your holiday baking, mix your cookie dough, pack it in a tightly covered container (or roll and wrap it as directed), and store it in the refrigerator for up to a week.

FREEZING COOKIES AND DOUGH

Most cookies freeze well. Freeze them in layers separated by a sheet of waxed paper. To thaw, let the cookies stand about 15 minutes in the container at room temperature.

Freeze cookies unfrosted because the frosting may cause the cookies to stick to one another. Also, cookies tend to absorb moisture from the frosting and lose their crispness.

If you plan to freeze bar cookies, before baking line the baking pan with foil, leaving 2 inches extra at each end. Add the batter, bake, and cool the bars in the lined pan as directed. Lift the foil to remove the cooled bars. Wrap in foil, seal, and freeze. Frost and cut the bars after thawing.

To freeze cookie dough, pack it in freezer containers. (For sliced cookies, roll and wrap the dough as directed in the recipe.) Freeze cookie dough for up to six months. Before baking, thaw frozen dough in the container in the refrigerator. If the dough is too stiff to work with, let the dough stand at room temperature to soften.

Baking on High

Living in the mountains may offer majestic views but can wreak havoc with your cookies. If you dwell at a high altitude (over 3,000 feet) and have difficulty getting your cookies to come out perfectly, try making these adjustments:
- Increase the oven temperature by 25° and slightly decrease the baking time (try 1 to 2 minutes).
- Reduce the sugar slightly (by just a couple of tablespoons to start).
- If a recipe calls for baking powder or soda, reduce the amount (by ⅛ teaspoon).
- For more information, contact your county extension agent or write: Colorado State University Food Science Extension Office, Fort Collins, CO 80523-1571.

HANDLE WITH CARE

Even the Scrooge on your Christmas gift list will rejoice in a parcel of homemade cookies. For faraway friends and family, a tin of homemade goodies makes a charming gift. Here are some hints for sending cookies by mail.

- Choose sturdy cookies that can travel well. Most bars or soft, moist cookies are good choices. Frosting or fillings may soften, causing cookies to stick together or to the wrapping.
- Wrap cookies back to back in pairs or individually with plastic wrap.
- Choose a heavy box and line it with plastic wrap or foil. Place a generous layer of filler, such as plastic bubble wrap, foam packing pieces, crumpled waxed paper, or paper towels on the bottom of the box.
- Layer the cookies and filler. Top the last cookie layer with plenty of filler to prevent the contents from shifting during shipping.

SOURCES

The following specialty shops and mail-order businesses are great resources for any baking and/or decorating supplies you might need as you embark on the Christmas cookie baking season.

■ **The Baker's Catalogue**
(by King Arthur's Flour)
P.O. Box 876
Norwich, VT 05055-0876
Phone: 800/827-6836

Baking supplies and ingredients, including edible decorations.

■ **Country Kitchen, SweetArt, Inc.**
3225 Wells St.
Ft. Wayne, IN 46808
Phone: 219/482-4835
Fax: 219/483-4091

Cake and cookie decorating supplies, including edible decorations.

■ **The House on the Hill**
P.O. Box 7003
Villa Park, IL 60181
Phone: 630/969-2624
Web site:
www.houseonthehill.net

Collection of imported and domestic springerle molds. Send $2.00 for a catalog.

■ **The Little Fox Factory**
931 Marion Rd.
Bucyrus, OH 44820
Send a stamped, self-addressed business-size envelope for a brochure.

■ **Sweet Celebration**
P.O. Box 39426
Edina, MN 55439-0426
Phone: 800/328-6722

Cookie cutters, decorating supplies, edible sprinkles, food coloring, baking equipment, cookie molds, stamps, presses, etc.

■ **N.Y. Cake and Baking**
Phone: 800/942-2539
Baking and decorating supplies, including neon food coloring.

■ **Sur La Table**
Catalogue Division
1765 Sixth Ave. S
Seattle, WA 98134-1608
Phone: 800/243-0852

Fine-quality baking equipment for domestic and professional kitchens.

■ **Wilton Enterprises**
2240 W. 75th St.
Woodridge, IL 60517
Phone: 800/794-5866
Web site: www.wilton.com

Cookie cutters, food coloring, decorating supplies, cake and cookie baking supplies. Their products can also be found in large chain retail stores.

■ **Williams-Sonoma**
Mail Order Department
P.O. Box 7456
San Francisco, CA 94120-7456
Phone: 800/541-2233
Fax: 800/541-1262

Fine-quality baking equipment and ingredients.

ORGANIZE A COOKIE EXCHANGE

Imagine starting the day with a plate piled high with gingerbread cookies and ending it with a collection of springerle, chocolate chippers, sugar cutouts, shortbread, and fruit-filled spirals. That's just what happens when you participate in a cookie exchange. A cookie exchange can be a large organized affair with dozens of participants, perhaps held to raise funds for a church or school. Or, you can plan a small gathering with a handful of friends in your home.

THE CONCEPT

The concept is simple. Maybe you have a group of friends who want a variety of cookies but don't have a lot of time to spend baking. A small cookie exchange in someone's home can satisfy their cookie wish lists. For an informal cookie exchange, each person brings one or two dozen cookies to share. (For a fund-raiser or larger event, ask participants to supply two to three dozen cookies.) Everyone goes home with the same number of cookies as they brought. The benefit: More varieties to enjoy!

HOLDING A FUND-RAISER

As with any endeavor, the success of a cookie exchange fund-raiser requires careful planning.

■ *Plan the Objective.* A cookie exchange for a larger group requires more organizing. Consider charging admission or holding a bake sale. Ask everyone to bring an extra dozen cookies to sell.

■ *Find a Location.* You'll need a large room with plenty of tables. Access to a kitchen area is helpful, especially if you plan to serve refreshments.

■ *Set the Date.* Be sure to give plenty of notice. Evenings and weekend afternoons book up quickly between Thanksgiving and Christmas, so for maximum participation, spread the word as early as the first of November. People will want plenty of time to bake their specialties.

■ *Spread the Word.* Create a flier and news release to promote the cookie exchange. Include details about the event such as the date, time, place, and what people need to bring—a few dozen cookies and a container to transport their cookies home, a phone number in case people want recipes or additional directions, and the name of the recipe written on a notecard, for example. Include information on how the proceeds will be used. Send your news release to the local media.

■ *Enlist Help.* Organize a committee of volunteers to carry out necessary responsibilities. You'll need helpers to set up tables, serve refreshments, and clean up.

EXCHANGE DAY

The set-up committee should arrive an hour or two before the cookie exchange. This will allow ample time for them to set up and decorate the room. Cover the tables with inexpensive paper tablecloths. Bring plenty of paper plates, aluminum foil or plastic wrap for everyone to wrap their goodies, and paper towels and garbage bags for clean up. As people arrive with their cookies, place their platters or tins of cookies on the tables, allowing enough room to move from one platter to the next.

■ *Stay on schedule.* Start the exchange no more than 15 minutes after the designated time.

When it's time to begin, choose someone from your committee with a good speaking voice to explain the process. Remind everyone they are to take home the same number of cookies they brought. You might want to set a limit on the number of cookies people may take from any one selection (four to six is a good number).

Be sure someone is available throughout the cookie exchange to answer questions and direct any latecomers. After the cookie exchange, the clean up committee should make sure the room is left as it was found, with all garbage placed in the trash cans. You may need to use the room again in the future—you'll want to make sure you are welcome!

INDEX

A

METRIC COOKING HINTS

By making a few conversions, cooks in Australia, Canada, and the United Kingdom can use these recipes with confidence. The charts on this page provide a guide for converting measurements from the U.S. customary system, which is used throughout this book, to the imperial and metric systems. There also is a conversion table for oven temperatures to accommodate the differences in oven calibrations.

Product Differences: Most of the ingredients called for in the recipes in this book are available in English-speaking countries. However, some are known by different names. Here are some common American ingredients and their possible counterparts:

- Sugar is granulated or castor sugar.
- Powdered sugar is icing sugar.
- All-purpose flour is plain household flour or white flour. When self-rising flour is used in place of all-purpose flour in a recipe that calls for leavening, omit the leavening agent (baking soda or baking powder) and salt.
- Light-colored corn syrup is golden syrup.
- Cornstarch is cornflour.
- Baking soda is bicarbonate of soda.
- Vanilla is vanilla essence.
- Golden raisins are sultanas.

Volume and Weight: Americans traditionally use cup measures for liquid and solid ingredients. The chart, above right, shows the approximate imperial and metric equivalents. If you are accustomed to weighing solid ingredients, the following approximate equivalents will be helpful.

- 1 cup butter, castor sugar, or rice = 8 ounces = about 250 grams
- 1 cup flour = 4 ounces = about 125 grams
- 1 cup icing sugar = 5 ounces = about 150 grams

  Spoon measures are used for smaller amounts of ingredients. Although the size of the tablespoon varies slightly in different countries, for practical purposes and for recipes in this book, a straight substitution is all that's necessary.

  Measurements made using cups or spoons always should be level unless stated otherwise.

EQUIVALENTS: U.S. = AUSTRALIA/U.K.

⅛ teaspoon = 0.5 ml
¼ teaspoon = 1 ml
½ teaspoon = 2 ml
1 teaspoon = 5 ml
1 tablespoon = 1 tablespoon
¼ cup = 4 tablespoons = 2 fluid ounces = 60 ml
⅓ cup = ¼ cup = 3 fluid ounces = 90 ml
½ cup = ⅓ cup = 4 fluid ounces = 120 ml
⅔ cup = ½ cup = 5 fluid ounces = 150 ml
¾ cup = ⅔ cup = 6 fluid ounces = 180 ml
1 cup = ¾ cup = 8 fluid ounces = 240 ml
1¼ cups = 1 cup
2 cups = 1 pint
1 quart = 1 liter
½ inch = 1.27 cm
1 inch = 2.54 cm

BAKING PAN SIZES

American	Metric
8×1½-inch round baking pan	20×4-cm cake tin
9×1½-inch round baking pan	23×3.5-cm cake tin
11×7×1½-inch baking pan	28×18×4-cm baking tin
13×9×2-inch baking pan	30×20×3-cm baking tin
2-quart rectangular baking dish	30×20×3-cm baking tin
15×10×1-inch baking pan	30×25×2-cm baking tin (Swiss roll tin)
9-inch pie plate	22×4- or 23×4-cm pie plate
7- or 8-inch springform pan	18- or 20-cm springform or loose-bottom cake tin
9×5×3-inch loaf pan	23×13×7-cm or 2-pound narrow loaf tin or pâté tin
1½-quart casserole	1.5-liter casserole
2-quart casserole	2-liter casserole

OVEN TEMPERATURE EQUIVALENTS

Fahrenheit Setting	Celsius Setting*	Gas Setting
300°F	150°C	Gas Mark 2 (slow)
325°F	160°C	Gas Mark 3 (moderately slow)
350°F	180°C	Gas Mark 4 (moderate)
375°F	190°C	Gas Mark 5 (moderately hot)
400°F	200°C	Gas Mark 6 (hot)
425°F	220°C	Gas Mark 7
450°F	230°C	Gas Mark 8 (very hot)
Broil		Grill

*Electric and gas ovens may be calibrated using Celsius. However, for an electric oven, increase the Celsius setting 10 to 20 degrees when cooking above 160°C. For convection or forced-air ovens (gas or electric), lower the temperature setting 10°C when cooking at all heat levels.

EMERGENCY BAKING SUBSTITUTION

If you're up to your elbows in flour when you discover you're out of an ingredient, you may not be out of luck. Sometimes another ingredient may be used in instead. Use these alternate ingredients only in a pinch, as they may affect the flavor and texture of your cookies.

If you don't have:	Substitute:
Apple pie spice, 1 teaspoon	½ teaspoon ground cinnamon plus ¼ teaspoon ground nutmeg, ⅛ teaspoon ground allspice, and dash ground cloves or ginger
Baking powder, 1 teaspoon	½ teaspoon cream of tartar plus ¼ teaspoon baking soda
Buttermilk, 1 cup	Sour milk: 1 tablespoon lemon juice or vinegar plus enough milk to make 1 cup (let stand 5 minutes before using); or 1 cup plain yogurt
Chocolate, semisweet, 1 ounce	3 tablespoons semisweet chocolate pieces; or 1 ounce unsweetened chocolate plus 1 tablespoon sugar
Chocolate, sweet baking, 4 ounces	¼ cup unsweetened cocoa powder plus ⅓ cup sugar and 3 tablespoons shortening
Chocolate, unsweetened, 1 ounce	3 tablespoons unsweetened cocoa powder plus 1 tablespoon cooking oil or shortening, melted
Egg, 1 whole	2 egg whites; 2 egg yolks; or ¼ cup frozen egg product, thawed
Flour, cake, 1 cup	1 cup minus 2 tablespoons all-purpose flour
Flour, self-rising, 1 cup	1 cup all-purpose flour plus 1 teaspoon baking powder, ½ teaspoon salt, and ¼ teaspoon baking soda
Ginger, fresh, grated, 1 teaspoon	¼ teaspoon ground ginger
Half-and-half or light cream, 1 cup	1 tablespoon melted butter or margarine plus enough whole milk to make 1 cup
Mascarpone cheese, 8 ounces	8 ounces regular cream cheese
Milk, 1 cup	½ cup evaporated milk plus ½ cup water; or 1 cup water plus ⅓ nonfat dry milk powder
Pumpkin pie spice, 1 teaspoon	½ teaspoon ground cinnamon plus ¼ teaspoon ground ginger, ¼ teaspoon ground allspice, and ⅛ teaspoon ground nutmeg
Sour cream, dairy, 1 cup	1 cup plain yogurt
Sugar, granulated, 1 cup	1 cup packed brown sugar